The Lord's Day, From Neither Catholics Nor Pagans

D. M. Canright, Fleming H. Revell Company

Copyright © BiblioLife, LLC

This book represents a historical reproduction of a work originally published before 1923 that is part of a unique project which provides opportunities for readers, educators and researchers by bringing hard-to-find original publications back into print at reasonable prices. Because this and other works are culturally important, we have made them available as part of our commitment to protecting, preserving and promoting the world's literature. These books are in the "public domain" and were digitized and made available in cooperation with libraries, archives, and open source initiatives around the world dedicated to this important mission.

We believe that when we undertake the difficult task of re-creating these works as attractive, readable and affordable books, we further the goal of sharing these works with a global audience, and preserving a vanishing wealth of human knowledge.

Many historical books were originally published in small fonts, which can make them very difficult to read. Accordingly, in order to improve the reading experience of these books, we have created "enlarged print" versions of our books. Because of font size variation in the original books, some of these may not technically qualify as "large print" books, as that term is generally defined; however, we believe these versions provide an overall improved reading experience for many.

The Lord's Day

From Neither Catholics nor Pagans

An Answer to Seventh-Day Adventism on this Subject

By

REV. D. M. CANRIGHT

Pastor Emeritus of the Berean Baptist Church, Grand Rapids, Mich., Author of "Seventh-Day Adventism Renounced," "Adventism Refuted in Ten Tracts," "Bible from Heaven," etc.

"I try to put myself in the place of the man who does not know all the things that I know."—*Pres. Woodrow Wilson.*

"We also are compassed about with so great a cloud of witnesses."—*Hebrews xii. 1.*

SECOND EDITION

NEW YORK   CHICAGO   TORONTO
Fleming H. Revell Company
LONDON   AND   EDINBURGH

My Present Standing.

When a prominent man leaves one church or party and joins an opposing one and gives his reasons for it he may expect that his old associates will reply to him. I expected no exception in my case when I renounced Adventism, so have not been disappointed. The great majority of my former brethren have been very friendly to me and treated me kindly. A few, a very few, have done otherwise. Their object has been to counteract my influence against what they regard as God's work. These few have started the report that I have been sorry I left Adventism, that I have said so, have tried to return to them, have confessed that my book was false, and some have said that I was very poor, a physical and mental wreck, with no hope of salvation, etc. These reports are accepted as facts by honest brethren and repeated till they are believed by many Adventists the world over. I have denied them in every possible way, but they are still believed and repeated, and doubtless always will be. I leave God to judge between us.

I now and here for the hundredth time solemnly affirm before God that I renounced Adventism because I believed it to be an error. I have never once regretted that I did so, have never intimated to any one that I have had the least desire to go back to that people. It would be impossible for me to do such a thing and be an honest man. I am now (1915) well in body and mind, have a good home worth $10,000 or $12,000, and have four grown children, of whom any man would be proud. On leaving the Adventists I joined the Baptist church at Otsego, Mich., and became its pastor till it was built up into a prosperous church. They have been my ardent friends to this day. Twenty years ago I moved to Grand Rapids, Mich., took a new mission and built this up, organized it into a church which has become one of the strong churches of the city, having several hundred members with a fine edifice. Have twice been its pastor, always an active member. At present I teach a large adult Bible class every Lord's day and often preach for them. Have always been in perfect harmony with the church. They honor me as their father, consult me on all important matters, and hotly resent the foolish reports which some circulate concerning me.

Out of scores of printed testimonies before me I select only a few which speak for themselves:

"*Grand Rapids, Mich., Nov. 1, 1907.*
"*To whom it may concern:*

"Having received many letters from all parts of the United States from those that have been informed by Adventists that Rev. D. M. Canright was not a member of a Baptist church and many other things pertaining to his character, we very emphatically denounce any such statements and will say that he is now and has been for many years an active member of the Berean Baptist church of this city and twice its pastor, a man above reproach and above all a noble Christian.

"Respectfully, W. H. Adrews, former clerk and charter member of the above named church. I hereby certify to the above.

"Rev. Robert Gray,
"Pastor of the Berean Church."

"*Grand Rapids, Mich., April 9, 1910.*
"*To whom it may concern, world wide,*
"DEAR BRETHREN:
"This letter is to say that Rev. D. M. Canright has been known to the undersigned for many years as an earnest, consecrated Christian man, and a true minister of Jesus Christ. He has been 'a faithful and true witness' against the errors of the Seventh-Day Adventists in his books and tracts for many years.

"OLIVER W. VAN OSDEL,
"Moderator Grand River Valley Association.
"ALEXANDER DODDS,
"President City Baptist Mission Society.
"W. I. COBURN,
"President Baptist Ministers' Conference."

The Baptists are not the only people who think well of the Rev. Mr. Canright. A Congregational minister adds his word:

"This certifies that I have been acquainted with the Rev. D. M. Canright of this city for more than forty-five years. At least twenty years of that time he was an Adventist preacher, and during those years his reputation as a Christian man and as a preacher of rare ability was of the highest order. His name among the Adventist people of this state was of the highest order. His name among the Adventist people of this state was a household word for righteousness of character, and an able defender of their faith. And when he left the Adventist denomination, all who knew the man, if they were at all imbued with the Christian spirit, must admit that the change made by him was due to a candid, conscientious conviction of what he believed to be right. There could be no other motive in his case, for he was successful beyond many of his brethren, and honored by them in the highest degree. For at least twenty years he and his beloved family have lived in this city and he has maintained the same reputation that he had, as a Christian gentleman and respected citizen. What I have written is from personal knowledge of Rev. D. M. Canright and of the Adventist denomination in this state.

"J. T. HUSTED,
"Pastor of the Wallin Congregational Church.
"*Grand Rapids, Mich.,
April 12, 1910.*"

The Methodist pastors add their tribute as follows:

"Various inquiries having come to the different members of the Association concerning the character and standing of Rev. D. M. Canright, the regular monthly meeting of the Methodist Ministers' Association of Grand Rapids, Mich., did, by an unanimous vote, adopt the following expression of its confidence in and regard for the personal worth and ministerial usefulness of Brother Canright.

"Rev. D. M. Canright, formerly a minister in the Seventh-Day Adventist Association, more recently a minister in the Baptist Association of this city, has been known by some of our number in person for several years and by reputation by the rest, and all our knowledge and information concerning him are of the most favorable kind.

"Any reflections on his personal character as a man, a husband, a citizen, a son or a Christian are without foundation, in fact, are unwarranted by any facts known to his intimate acquaintances. He is honored among his brethren, respected in his own community, and is commended by us as being worthy of confidence and trust.

He has had an honored and useful ministry, and in no sense is deserving of the attacks made on him.

"Done at Grand Rapids, Mich., this 11th day of April, 1910, by the authority of the Grand Rapids Methodist Ministers' Association, by

"JOHN R. T. LATHROP, District Supt.
"CHARLES NEASE, President.
"J. R. WOOTEN, Secretary."

"*Grand Rapids, Mich., April 11, 1910.*

"It is with sincere pleasure that I write concerning the character and integrity of the Rev. D. M. Canright. I have known him and his family a good many years, and do not hesitate to say that they are very estimable people, and have the confidence of their neighbors and friends in the community.

"I consider Mr. Canright a Christian gentleman in every sense of the word; a man of the highest integrity and one who desires, in every project with which he is connected, to make righteousness his guide to action.

"He has done business with our bank for a good many years and I have personally had reason to test his integrity and am unequivocal in my expression of confidence in him.

"Very truly yours,
"CHARLES W. GARFIELD."

(Mr. Garfield is president of a bank with $2,000,000.)

Adventists sometimes say I left them four or five times. I withdrew from that church just once, no more, that was final. Their church records at Battle Creek and Otsego will show that. For years I was troubled with doubts about some of their doctrines and three times stopped preaching for a short period, but remained a member in good standing. At a large camp-meeting I was persuaded to swallow my doubts, take up the work again, confess that I had been in the dark, and go on again. I yielded my judgment to the entreaties of my brethren and the love I had for old associates and said what I soon regretted. I found it a terrible struggle to break away from what had held me so long.

Since I left them they try to make it appear that I did not amount to much anyway. "Sour grapes," said the fox to the delicious fruit which he could not reach! As a refutation of their detractions, see Chapter II of my book. I will here state only a few facts briefly:

During two years, 1876, 1877, I was one of the general conference committee of three which had control of all their work in the world. There is no higher authority in the denomination. How did it happen that I was placed in that office if I was not one of their best men? Year after year I was elected on the boards having charge of their most important institutions, such as their Publishing House, College, Sanitarium, Sabbath School Association, etc., etc. For proof of this see their printed year books where my name appear constantly. I was made theological teacher in their college, president of a state conference, associate editor of a paper, etc. I selected and arranged the course of reading which all their ministers had to follow, and I was sent to their annual state conferences to examine these preachers in those studies, in their theology, and in their fitness for the ministry. Is such work usually committed to an inferior man?

But it was as a writer in their papers, as the author of numerous tracts, pamphlets and books covering nearly every controverted point of their faith, as a lecturer and debater in defense of their doctrines, that I was the best known during the last fifteen years I was with them. In these lines, not a man among them stood as prominent as I did. Every one at all familiar with their work during that period knows that I tell only the simple truth in the case. They know it, too. For my writings the office once paid me $500 in one check and many other times different sums. After twenty-seven years they still publish and use several of my tracts as being better than anything they have been able to produce since.

My long and thorough acquaintance with Adventism and all their arguments prepared me to answer them as no other could. Hundreds of ministers from all parts have written me their thanks for the aid my book has been to them in meeting Adventism. Did not God in his providence prepare me for this work? I humbly believe he did, and this reconciles me to the long and bitter experiences I had in that bondage. But if God and the truth is honored, I am content.

The only question is, do I know their doctrines well enough to state them clearly, and have I the ability to answer them plainly? Let my work be the answer.

Since I withdrew Adventists have published five or six different tracts to head off my influence. If I amount to so little, why all this effort? What they do refutes what they say. God has preserved me to outlive nearly all the Adventist ministers with whom I began laboring. At seventy-five am full of faith in God and the hope of eternal life through our Lord Jesus Christ.

I love those brethren still and know that most of them are honest Christian people, but in error on many of their views. I would be glad to help them if I could.

D. M. CANRIGHT,
Pastor Emeritus of the Berean Baptist Church.
Grand Rapids, Michigan.

THE Berean Baptist Church was raised up by Elder Canright and organized June 5, 1892, with fifty members. Since then four hundred and fifty have been baptized into the church. It has prospered steadily from the first. Its membership now is three hundred and thirty-one and steadily increasing. Its location is one of the best in our city of 120,000. It has a good church edifice with all modern conveniences and is clear of debt. In the city and state it is recognized as one among the most alive, aggressive, and strictly evangelical Baptist churches.

The church has always acknowledged with gratitude the work Elder Canright did under God in starting it on a solid Scriptural foundation, which it has always zealously maintained.

A. J. BUSH, *Church Clerk*,
Berean Baptist Church.

September 23, 1915.

Preface

ONE of the chief things which Seventh-Day Adventists urge the most strongly is that the observance of Sunday originated with the pagan Romans, thence was brought into the Roman Church and then the Pope, or the Papacy, imposed this upon the entire Christian world. Hence Sunday is only a pagan, papal day. They assert this so strongly and so repeatedly, that uninformed people are frightened into giving up the Lord's Day and accepting instead the Jewish Sabbath. It is a subject on which people are generally not posted. Even those who are intelligent and well read on general topics know little, or nothing, on this particular subject, while the common people know absolutely nothing about it.

To learn the real facts in the case requires much careful research in the history of both Church and State through several centuries of the early Church. Few people have the time, or the means at hand, or the interest to do all this. Even educated ministers in general have never given the subject much thought, because they have had no occasion to do so. Hence, when suddenly required to meet Adventists on this question, they are unprepared, nor do they have the necessary authorities at hand to quickly look it up. So the strong assertions of the Adventists often go unanswered. In an ordinary audience of several hundred there would not be one person who would know how the pagan Romans regarded Sunday, or whether the Papacy ever had anything to do with it or not. Hence they are easily misled.

I do not mean to accuse the Adventists of purposely deceiving. I myself taught that way for many years while with them. I accepted what our own "History of the Sabbath" said, and quoted it as conclusive. It was long before I saw how one-sided it was.

In this present book both ministers and common people will have the facts in concise and handy form for ready reference with the testimony of the most reliable and unbiased authorities given in their own words.

I made several typewritten copies of the manuscript and sent them to five well-informed ministers, requesting each one to spare no criticism nor pass over any questionable point. Together they gave me valuable help and eliminated some non-essentials. They also added much of value which I had not found myself. All these I gladly accepted.

Rev. John J. Husted, Congregationalist, had been familiar with Adventists for fifty years. Rev. O. W. Van Osdell, D. D., Baptist, had met their arguments often.

Rev. M. H. McLeod, Presbyterian, has published

a written discussion with a prominent defender of Adventism.

Rev. W. H. Phelps, Methodist, had been for seven years pastor of the M. E. Church in Battle Creek, Mich., and was at the time in a discussion with the Adventist's pastor. Hence, all were well qualified to judge of the matter in my manuscript. Read their commendations on a previous page.

Then I selected a Seventh-Day Adventist minister, one of the most critical students in their ranks. He kindly consented to criticize my manuscripts. He did a thorough job, cutting out, or adding words and sentences, or pointing out what he thought were objectionable statements. I gladly accepted nearly all the criticisms he made and omitted some things which he questioned. I greatly valued his review of the work. I did not expect him to agree with all my conclusions nor recommend the book. He could not do this and remain a Seventh-Day Adventist. His criticisms were all made in a friendly tone, showing that a kindliness of spirit is not all on one side.

For myself, after thorough research, I am profoundly satisfied that the Christian Church has been right in observing the Lord's Day. I have written this work with constant prayer that I might be fair and kind in my statements. I have a high regard for my Advent brethren, and the most kindly feeling towards them.

I know they are sincere, but am sure they are

mistaken in their views about the Sabbath and the Lord's Day. Their wide-spread and aggressive agitation of these subjects will result in a better understanding of these questions.

This book is not written to convert Adventists, but to defend our own faith. If they would let our members alone, we would say nothing; but we would be recreant to our duty if we kept still while they publicly denounce us as pagans and papists and then go from house to house among our Christian members with their literature and Bible readings to proselyte them to their erroneous views.

The future of Seventh-Day Adventism,—what will it be? This is a conundrum. Apparently two insurmountable difficulties lie before them in the near future.

First. They are now, 1915, putting tremendous emphasis on their claim that the end must, and will, come in the generation beginning in 1844, now seventy-one years in the past. They say they are now "finishing the work," "just entering the port." It creates great enthusiasm, large gifts, and big sacrifices. But if the generation passes, if a few decades come and go, then what? Yes, then what? Must not a sad catastrophe follow?

Second. From the beginning, they have claimed that their "Message" is to gather out just the 144,000 of Rev. vii. 1-4; xiv. 1-5. Then the end will come. But they now have 122,000. As they are gaining now, two or three years more will complete the number wanted. Then what? Suppose, after a few years, they number 200,000, or 56,000 more than wanted, then what? Yes, then what?

Third. Another issue confronts them: A younger generation is arising in the Church, better educated, more intelligent, more cultured, and more tolerant towards other Churches. These are steadily, but surely, adopting the manners and methods of the older Churches. These young men are beginning quietly to discount Mrs. White, and do a little independent thinking for themselves.

Will these be strong enough to leaven the body, or will they split the Church on some new issue now that Mrs. White is dead?

After I left them, naturally, my Advent brethren expected that the frown of God would follow me for opposing their "message." Hence ever since it is reported among them that I have become a physical and mental wreck, poverty poor, in despair spiritually, etc. But the fact is that at the age of seventy-five I am in perfect health, have the same strong faith and hope in God as ever. Financially am better off than ever before. As to my mental conditions let these pages answer.

I have outlived nearly all the Advent ministers who labored with me. Elder White died at the early age of sixty; one of my age, with whom I labored, died some years ago insane; another companion-laborer was killed in the cars; another was drowned; and many more died very young. Had any of this happened to me it would have been reported as the judgment of God. Then my remarkable preservation and prosperity should be accredited to God's blessing. I firmly believe it that way.

Every page of this work has been written with earnest prayer that the tender spirit of the Master may breathe through it all. None of us is infallible. All are liable to make mistakes. Hence, we need to be charitable towards those who have the misfortune to be misled.

Contents

I. SEVENTH-DAY ADVENTISM — WHAT? WHENCE? WHITHER? . . . 31

Origin with Millerism in 1844—Sincere—Mrs. White their prophetess—Set Oct. 22, 1844 for the end—Contradicted Christ—Ten mistakes —Endorse Millerism—Call Churches "Babylon"—Probation ended in 1844—Adopt Jewish Sabbath — Proselyte — Exclusive — Church and state to unite—Predict triumph—The harm it does.

II. THE "RELIGIOUS LIBERTY" SCARECROW   54

Persecution predicted—Death penalty—World-wide—United States to lead—All nations to keep Sunday—Impossible theory—All the trend the other way—Persecution dying out— Mrs. White commands them to keep Sunday— Sunday laws do not affect religious liberty— Affects civil liberty only—Illustrated—They use worldly political methods.

III. ADVENTISTS ASSERT THAT THE CATHOLIC CHURCH CHANGED THE SABBATH; BUT WHICH CATHOLIC CHURCH? 74

Advent assertions—Roman Church—Claims origin with apostles—Date of first "Pope" —"Catholic" Church, "Roman Church," "Papacy," all different—True Catholic Church Apostolic—This is not the Roman Church, but the general Church—The Eastern Greek Church, not Rome, is the "Mother Church."

IV. CATHOLICS LOCATE THE CHANGE OF THE SABBATH BACK WITH THE APOSTLES . 87

This is the doctrine of the Roman Church— Council of Trent—Catholic Bible—Papal delegate—Cardinal Gibbons—Archbishop Ireland—Catholic Encyclopedia—Catholic Dictionary—Written testimony of two Catholic priests—Catechisms—Mission priests—Catholic "Challenges."

V. THE PAGAN ROMANS AND GREEKS HAD NO WEEKLY DAY OF REST, OR FESTIVAL, OR WORSHIP . . . 102

Advent Theory—Claim pagans kept Sunday as a festival—Papacy brought it into the Church—The theory false—Testimony of British Museum — Smithsonian Institute — Harvard University —Wisconsin University—Fowler's Roman Festival text book—Standard Dictionary — Webster — Max Muller—Tertullian—Encyclopedias — Dr. Schaff — Admissions of Adventists themselves—No heathen nation ever kept Sunday—Lord's Day did not originate with pagans, but with Christians.

VI. HISTORICAL EVIDENCE THAT OUR LORD'S DAY WAS OBSERVED FROM THE TIME OF THE APOSTLES . . 129

Pliny's Letter—Barnabas—Teachings of the Apostles — Justin Martyr — Bardesanese — Clement — Tertullian — Origen — Apostolical Constitutions — Cyprian —Athanasius—Laodicea—Augustine—The Greek Church—Cyclopedias—The Jewish Sabbath not kept.

VII. SUNDAY OBSERVANCE ORIGINATED WITH THE EASTERN, OR GREEK CHURCH, NOT WITH ROME IN THE WEST . 165

The Church began in the East, not in Rome, in the West, Eastern Church the Mother—Rome the Daughter—Testimony of Bishop Raphael—Greek catechism — Gospel carried from Greece to Rome—East to West, not from Rome East—Greek Church largest, most influential for centuries—Rome no influence on East—Thirty facts in favor of—Five great gospel memorials—Easter controversy.

CONTENTS

VIII.	CONSTANTINE'S SUNDAY LAW, A. D. 321	188

Constantine's parents Christians—His conversion in 312—His edict nine years later—Proof—Only a civil law—First Civil Law for Sunday rest — Eusebius — Constantine's policy—Summary—Testimony of Adventists.

IX.	THE LORD'S DAY AT THE COUNCILS OF NICE, A. D. 325, AND LAODICEA, A. D. 364	205

The Lord's Day recognized by the first general council—Importance of that council—Sabbath ignored—Jewish Sabbath condemned at Laodicea and the Lord's Day sustained—It was wholly a Greek council—not Roman.

X.	THE PAPACY AND THE LORD'S DAY	219

Adventists' assertions—The Papacy wholly a Western institution—No authority for centuries after Christ—Testimony of encyclopedias—Of Adventists themselves—Lord's Day kept centuries before the Papacy was founded—Had no influence in the East—No Papacy in the East—Admission of Adventists—Eastern Church opposed to Rome—"The Spirit of the Papacy."

XI.	THE MARK OF THE BEAST—WHAT IS IT?	232

Adventists say it is Sunday-keeping—That theory absurd—The Mark of the Papacy is the supremacy of the Pope.

XII.	THE TEN COMMANDMENTS NOT CHANGED BY CATHOLICS—ADVENTISTS DECAPITATE THE DECALOGUE	247

How Adventists try to prove it—Protestant and Catholic Catechisms compared—Lutheran Catechism—Adventists decapitate the Decalogue—Introductory words important part of that law and designate the Author of it.

I

SEVENTH-DAY ADVENTISM—WHAT? WHENCE? WHITHER?

TO know Adventism better than Adventists know it themselves! That is no small claim, and the reader must judge as to whether this claim is made good. I believe in, and love, the doctrine of the Second Advent of Christ, and with many others, hope it is near. I only wish to guard against false theories concerning it.

Having spent twenty-eight years of the best of my life among a people who initiated this form of faith, or have espoused it, and having given my services to them and for them for that period of time, I may modestly claim that I may be credited with a knowledge of that whereof I speak.

NOTE.—In this chapter I design to give only such a brief outline of Seventh-Day Adventism as will enable the reader to comprehend why this book is written. For a full account of this peculiar tenet of faith, and for an answer to the arguments of its advocates from the Bible, see my other book, as announced on the front page.

The facts concisely stated in this chapter may all be found in full in books bearing the imprimatur of Seventh-Day Adventism itself. See "Early Writings," by Mrs. White; Life of Miller; Life of Elder White; "Great Controversy," by Mrs. White, and their Year Book for any year. All these may be ordered from Adventist publishing houses.

The adherents of Seventh-Day Adventism are to be commended for their strong faith in God, in the Saviour, and in the Bible. They are ensamples in the great sacrifices they cheerfully make for their faith, and in their zeal for what they firmly believe to be the only message for this generation. Among them I have many good friends.

Their mistaken views, their excessive zeal for these views, and their general condemnation of others for not accepting them, largely counteracts the good they otherwise might do. These things, and some of the methods they employ in promulgating their doctrines, lead them to become very annoying to other Christians equally as devoted as themselves. I am sorry to say that, unknown to the great majority of their own people, their leaders have dissembled with regard to their past mistakes and their reliance upon Mrs. White's "inspiration." The laity, specially the converts in foreign lands, know nothing of this nor will they believe it.

While they hold and teach the fundamentals of Christian doctrines, with these they mix a large number of errors. These erroneous theories they make the most prominent in their work, urging them as the present *test* of acceptance with God. This does great harm. It is only these false teachings which I wish to answer. They base their special "message" upon their own peculiar interpretation of different lines of symbolical prophecies, with which no other expositors agree. It is a field where they can easily be mistaken as they have all along in their past history.

From the first, Mrs. White has been held as a prophetess and all her writings and teachings are regarded just as divinely inspired as the prophets of the Bible. Publicly, they try to soften this, but, privately, teach it strongly. No minister or editor is tolerated among them who questions it. To their own people they quote her as "inspiration," as the "voice of the Lord," on everything they wish to carry through, because she always has a ready revelation to fit that case. In their church papers she is quoted far more than the Bible. Here is one from the *Lake Union Herald*, November 7, 1914. It says: "Read carefully the following *written by the pen of inspiration*." Then follows a quotation from Mrs. White. Again: "As with the ancient prophets, the talking is done by the Holy Spirit *through her vocal organs*. The prophets spake as they were moved by the Holy Ghost—2 Peter i. 21."[1] No stronger possible endorsement of her inspiration could be made. She, herself, all through her writings, hundreds of times, makes the same claim. Hear her: "It is God, and not an erring mortal, that has spoken."[2] Mrs. White stands related to Seventh-Day Adventism the same as the Pope to Catholicism, or Mrs. Eddy to Christian Science. If you become a Seventh-Day Adventist, sooner or later, you will have to accept Mrs.

[1] *Review and Herald*, Oct. 5, 1914.
[2] "Testimonies," Vol. III, p. 257.

White's Testimonies as the voice of God or get out. She has written twenty volumes. They push the sale of these in every possible way, through their papers, catalogues, by ministers, canvassers, colporteurs, etc. But they have not one single person specially convassing or working to sell Bibles. This is significant.

During the past year many, both ministers and laymen, have been expelled from this Church because they refused to accept Mrs. White's Testimonies as inspired revelations.

For the same reason many Churches have been disbanded to get rid of these unbelievers in Mrs. White who could not be excommunicated any other way. Two papers are now published by these "Castouts."

It is remarkable what a large number has all along left the body on account of unbelief in Mrs. White's Testimonies. This includes many of their most talented ministers, editors, writers, college professors, physicians, and business managers. I could fill several pages with simply a list of their names. Every year sees new ones added to the list. Ten years hence some, who are now prominent in that Church, will be outside and opposing it, judging from the past. Many who have no real faith in Mrs. White's inspiration are held there by official position, faith in other parts of the doctrines, and dread of religious ostracism by their old associates. I have been there and know.

Modern Adventism of all branches originated

with one Wm. Miller, an old, uneducated farmer, a sincere Christian, but a visionary. Of him the "Schaff-Herzog Encyclopedia" says: "Limited in his educational advantages, and a farmer by occupation, he yet pretended to interpret prophecy." The same authority, article "Adventists," says: "Adventists, or the followers of Wm. Miller, a fanatical student who put the Second Advent of Christ in the year 1843." The unanimous opinion of the Christian world to-day agrees in this view of Miller. "Millerism" has become a byword of reproach ever since. Adventists themselves are ashamed of it; yet that was their origin.

Miller rejected all Biblical commentaries, simply took the Bible and wholly relied upon his own unaided views of it. He decided that all prophetic periods would end in 1843. A chart was prepared with all dates ending there, all signs fulfilled then. Adventists themselves have proved Miller unreliable because they find many prophecies not fulfilled even now, while he taught positively that all were fulfilled in 1843-1844.

Soon a number of ministers joined him in preaching that set time. Quite a number were converted to that view. But 1843 passed, and, of course, their predictions all failed. Learning nothing by this, the Adventists next set October 22, 1844, for the end of the world. Several hundreds went out "lecturing" on that "*time.*" Papers were published, and books and tracts were scattered widely. The work was largely confined to a few of the New

England and adjoining states with scattering ones elsewhere. Everywhere it was regarded as a religious freak and is still so regarded. Possibly forty or fifty thousand in all, for a period, favored that set time.

As they came near the day, great enthusiasm prevailed. Business ceased, goods were given away, crops were left ungathered, meetings were constantly held, and all were waiting for the end. No food even for the next day was provided. Of course, it failed again. Five years later Miller died a disappointed old man. Nearly all who took part in that work have passed away. But fanaticism dies hard and its sad fruits are here yet.

Over and over Jesus, in the plainest possible language, warned against just what Adventists did in 1843 and again in 1844—setting a definite time for the Lord to come. Hear Him: " But of that day and hour knoweth no man, no, not the angels of heaven, but My Father only." " Ye know not what hour your Lord doth come." " In such an hour as ye think not, the Son of man cometh " (Matt. xxiv. 36, 42, 44 ; also Matt. xxv. 13). Again: " Ye know not when the time is " (Mark xiii. 33 ; see also Acts i. 7).

The passing of their set time has proved their folly to all the world. Here is what they predicted to occur October 22, 1844:

1. Christ would come in the clouds of heaven.
2. All the angels would come with Him.
3. Gabriel's trumpet would sound.

4. Probation would end.
5. The dead saints would be raised.
6. The living saints would be changed.
7. The wicked dead would rise.
8. The earth would be cleansed by fire.
9. The wicked would be destroyed.
10. The saints would inherit the new earth.

Not one single thing of all this occurred—all failed. Now read Deut. xviii. 18: "When a prophet speaketh in the name of the Lord, if the thing follow not, not come to pass, that is the thing which the Lord hath not spoken." By this plain rule, the Advent preaching of 1844 was proved to be not of God.

As might have been expected, great confusion and all kinds of fanaticism followed. Adventists then split up into several different parties, opposing each other and continuing their divisions to this day. There are seven of these now. All these are the results of that time setting.

Such a brood of errors and heresies as has resulted from Millerism cannot be found in the history of the Church.

Take the matter of time-setting: some of these different parties of Adventists have set the time for the end of the world in 1843, 1844, 1847, 1850, 1852, 1854, 1855, 1863, 1866, 1867, 1868, 1877, and so on, till one is sick of counting. Learning nothing from the past, each time they are quite as confident as before.

This fanatical work has brought disgrace upon

the doctrine of the Second Advent, so that it is not now dwelt upon as much as formerly in other Churches. The study of the prophecies has been brought into disrepute by the unwise course of the Adventists. No thoughtful man can fail to see this.

To their credit it should be said that Seventh-Day Adventists do not believe in setting time definitely since 1844. But then their leaders were all in that particular time-setting and defend it yet. Elder White engaged in that time-setting in 1843 and 1844. So their leader was a time-setter. Mrs. White, their prophetess, was also engaged in the time-setting of 1843 and 1844.

Elders Bates, Andrews, Rhodes, and all the first crop of Seventh-Day Adventists were in the time-setting of 1843 and 1844 and these Adventists still defend it as right and approved of God. They claim to be simply carrying on the same work which Miller then began. In all their books and sermons they point to 1844 as their origin and endorse the work of the Millerites. The following from Mrs. White will settle the point: "I have seen that the 1843 chart was directed by the hand of the Lord, and that it should not be altered; that the figures were as He wanted them; that His hand was over and hid a mistake in some of the figures."[1] This endorses that work and throws upon God the blame of their blunder! It will be seen that Mrs. White in her "inspired" revela-

[1] "Early Writings," p. 64.

tions strongly endorsed Miller's figures for 1843–1844. All Seventh-Day Adventists have to abide by and defend these now, and always must in the future.

So their entire system rests upon the figures of an old farmer of seventy years ago and the visions of an uneducated girl in her teens! A very doubtful foundation. Out of this confusion came Seventh-Day Adventism this way:

Enthusiastically engaged in setting these two times were all their leaders. These persons held on to the time-setting of 1843–1844 as being right and of God; but said that on October 22, 1844, Christ, instead of coming to the earth, as they had preached, began the judgment of the world up in heaven! Now they had it where no one could go and report on facts and so were safe to speculate on new theories.

As all the Churches had opposed their work, they, in turn, denounced them all as fallen, rejected of God, apostates, and "Babylon." And this they have preached strongly ever since. In big letters they label all other Churches "*Babylon*," and cry, "Come out of her."

Thus Mrs. White: "As the Churches refused to receive the first angel's message [Miller's work] they rejected the light from heaven and fell from the favor of God."[1] Again Mrs. White says: "Satan has taken full possession of the Churches as a body. Their profession, their prayers, and their

[1] "Early Writings," p. 101.

exhortations are an abomination in the sight of God" (page 135). What awful thing had they done to fall so? Why, Miller said the world would end in 1844 and the Churches said it wouldn't. He was wrong and they were right, but God rejected them and upheld the Millerites!

This view of all Churches they still hold. Hence, of course, they can have no fellowship with them. So they are just as zealous to proselyte a devout member of a church as they are to preach to sinners.

PROBATION CLOSED IN 1844

Adventists adopted the view that probation for sinners and all the unconverted world ended in 1844. Mrs. White states it thus: "After the passing of the time of expectation in 1844, Adventists still believed the Saviour's coming to be very near; they held that the work of Christ as man's intercessor before God had ceased. Having given the warning of the judgment near, they felt that their work for the world was done, and they lost their burden of souls for the salvation of sinners. All this confirmed them in the belief that probation had ended, or, as they then expressed it, 'the door of mercy was shut.'"[1] This statement of Mrs. White herself is enough to settle the point that the Adventists believed "the door of mercy was shut" in 1844.

While Miller and all other Adventists soon abandoned this theory, Seventh-Day Adventists con-

[1] "Great Controversy," p. 268, edition 1884.

tinued to believe and teach it strongly for several years, or until 1851. Here are Mrs. White's own words:

"March 24, 1849. . . . I was shown that the commandments of God and the testimony of Jesus Christ, relating to the *shut door*, could not be separated. . . . I saw that the mysterious signs and wonders and false reformations would increase and spread. The reformations that were shown me were not reformations from error to truth, but from bad to worse, for those who professed a change of heart had only wrapped about them a religious garb, which covered up the iniquity of a wicked heart. Some appeared to have been really converted, so as to deceive God's people, but if their hearts could be seen they would appear as black as ever. My accompanying angel bade me look for the travail of soul for sinners as used to be. I looked, but could not see it, for the time for their salvation is past." [1]

Here you have the shut door and no mercy for sinners just as clear as language can make it. Every candid reader knows what it teaches.

"The Present Truth," James White, editor, Oswego, N. Y., May, 1850, has an article by the editor on the "Sanctuary, 2,300 Days, and the Shut Door." Elder White says: "At that point of time [1844] the midnight cry was given, the work for the world was closed up, and Jesus passed into the most holy place. . . . When we came up to

[1] "Present Truth," pp. 21-22, published August, 1849.

that point of time, all our sympathy, burden and prayers for sinners ceased, and the unanimous feeling and testimony was that our work for the world was finished forever." Any honest man can see that the "shut door" meant no salvation for sinners, and this is what Elder White and his wife taught up till 1851.

It will be seen that Seventh-Day Adventism was born in this monstrous delusion that probation for the world ended in 1844, over seventy years ago. Did God send people to preach such a fearful error as that? If they made such terrible mistakes then, are they safe to follow now?

If any of Mrs. White's revelations were from God, those teaching the close of probation for sinners in 1844 certainly were, for she states it in the most positive terms over and over during several years, or from 1844 to 1851. Her written revelations for those years are full of it. Her statements are too plain for denial. I have all of them here now. But neither she nor her people believe that theory now. This is positive proof that God never told her what she claimed back there. If she was misled and deceived then, she has never been reliable since. The entire Seventh-Day Advent message is so inseparably bound up with her revelations that they must stand or fall together.

In 1846 Elder White and wife were married, both young, she only nineteen, very sickly and claiming to have "visions." Soon Elders Bates, Holt,

Rhodes, Edson, and Andrews joined them. All these had been in the time-setting movement of 1843-1844. To their Advent theory they gradually added the visions as divine revelations, the Jewish Sabbath, sleep of the dead, annihilation of the wicked, feet-washing, tithing, a radical health-diet, a short dress with pants for women, and other peculiarities. They now claimed that they were raised up of God to preach the three messages of Rev. xiv. 6-14. The Jewish Sabbath is the chief thing. This is the "seal of God" with which the 144,000 of Revelation vii. are to be sealed for translation when Christ comes, which is right at hand. These 144,000, all of whom will be Seventh-Day Adventists, will be all the ones then living on the earth who will be saved. All others, Baptists, Methodists, Presbyterians, no matter what they profess, unless they join them before that time, will be lost. Hence, necessarily, they oppose all other Churches as "Babylon," will unite with none in any way, but zealously proselyte from all in every possible way, both at home and in all the missionary fields in heathen lands. A large percentage of their "converts" are from other Churches. In this way they work great confusion, specially in foreign mission fields among the simple minded native converts. Foreign missionaries report that this is becoming one of the great hindrances they have to meet.

I have letters from missionaries all over the world all agreeing in this.

A letter of April 9, 1914, by Bishop William Burt, Buffalo, N. Y., says: "In Europe, and especially in Italy, these Adventists have been a troublesome lot. After we have fished people out of sin and superstition they come around to trouble them with their doctrines."

Methodist Episcopal Church,
Inayat Bagh, Lucknow, India.

Dear Brother:

I knew Seventh-Day Adventists at home and have known much of them here, and it is my judgment that their methods are worse on the foreign field than at home. The new converts have never heard of such things as they teach, and they are confused before we can even find out that they are secretly sending their literature and their workers among our people.

Fraternally,
FRANK W. WARNE,
Missionary Bishop, Southern Asia.

Honolulu, T. H., March 21, 1911.

Dear Brother:

The Seventh-Day Adventists are proselyters rather than missionaries. Here in Hawaii they confine their efforts to such work among white people and Christian Japanese and Chinese, for whom missionaries have labored for years, and whose minds become greatly confused through the propaganda among these new converts.

Sincerely,
JOHN W. WADMAN,
Supt. Hawaii Mission, M. E. Church.

Edinburgh, Scotland.

Dear Brother:

The work of Seventh-Day Adventists in Japan and Korea is proselyting. They have divided Churches and paralyzed others, and have done much harm. This I am sorry to state, as some of their missionaries mean well.

Sincerely,
BISHOP HARRIS,
Missionary for Japan and Korea.

London, England, July 1, 1910.

Dear Brother:

It is painful for me to be obliged to write that our Seventh-Day Adventist friends are almost wholly engaged in proselyting from the evangelical mission. They are a sore trial to us in that they seem to delight in disrupting small groups of earnest Christians gathered with infinite toil from the heathen world around us.

Sincerely,
BISHOP W. H. OLDHAM,
M. E. Church.

*South America Mission of the
Methodist Episcopal Church.
Buenos Aires, May 16, 1911.*

Dear Brother:

Here Seventh-Day Adventists do not seem to do much work among the unconverted Romanists or unbelievers, but carry on an active propaganda of their specialty among those already in the evangelical church.

Yours fraternally,
SAMUEL P. CRAVER.

New York City, June 14, 1910.

Dear Brother:

The Seventh-Day Adventists are persistent propagandists as to their peculiar views, and I often wish they would give their force less to non-essentials in the matter of salvation, and unite upon the broad spiritual demand for salvation in Jesus Christ.

Sincerely yours,
JOSEPH C. HARTZELL,
Bishop of Africa M. E. Church.

Adventists themselves report the same as these other missionaries do. Thus: "A friend of mine visited the young people's services at the Tabernacle and heard a returned missionary from Africa tell how he had started his Mission near a Methodist chapel and how, in due season, he won every single member to the truth and forced the minister to close the doors and begin elsewhere. Here your missionaries and ours tell the same story" (Rev. W. H. Phelps, M. E. Pastor, Battle Creek, Mich.).

The following is from the *South African Sentinel*, an Adventist missionary paper:

"I am sorry to say, we have met some bitter opposition from one of the Churches. Six of our most promising people who belonged to, and attended, that Church kept the Sabbath for some time, but finally gave it up because of the efforts made by the ministers and through reading the Canright book denouncing Adventism."

It will be seen that they get their best members out of other Churches and then complain of "bitter opposition" from that Church!

Pearl Lagoon, Nicaragua.

Dear Sir:

Their way of working is here probably the same as elsewhere. They try to win over members of our own Church. I deeply regret their coming here, because we have still to deal with heathenism, and Adventists sow distrust against us. Missionaries of our Church have labored on this coast when it was almost unknown to the outside world.

Yours truly,
H. SCHUBERT.

It will be seen that Adventists are not welcome anywhere by Christian missionaries.

Mrs. White and their leaders dictate to their people the same exclusive system which Roman Catholics teach their members. Hear her: "I was shown the necessity of those who believe that we are having the last message of mercy being separate from those who are daily imbibing new errors. I saw that neither young nor old should attend their meetings. God is displeased with us when we go to listen to error without being obliged to go."[1]

Their editors enforce the same teachings. Thus Elder Uriah Smith says:

"It will not mix."

"That system of belief which we denominate the 'Present Truth' possesses this peculiar feature, that it will *not mix with anything else.* It is a

---

[1] "Early Writings," supplement pages 37, 38.

sharp, clean cut, decisive doctrine. It admits of no halving, no copartnership or compromise."[1] Both of these are like the language of a Roman Catholic priest to his members, and both are obeyed as implicitly. Hence, as a rule, they attend only their own meetings, hear only their own ministers, and read only their own religious literature. As a result they sincerely believe they are the only ones who have the truth, the only ones who have God's special favors! Mrs. White assumes to hold the *keys* to heaven as firmly as the Pope does. Reject her inspiration, her teachings, and you will never enter heaven!

They teach that Sunday is only a pagan day brought into the Church by the Roman Papacy, and is the mark of the beast, hateful to God. They are now called to restore the old Sabbath.

This is now "the seal of God" (Rev. vii. 1-8), with which 144,000 saints will be gathered out from "Babylon" and the world. The Sabbath is now the supreme *test* of loyalty to God. They are sent to "test" all with it. This will bring out 144,000 all perfect saints who will be living and translated when Jesus comes (Rev. xiv. 1-5). Of all the millions on earth at that time, in the Churches or out, not one will be saved except these 144,000, and all these will be keeping the Sabbath, —Seventh-Day Adventists! "The Biblical Institute," by Elder Uriah Smith, page 240 says: "We answer that before the end we understand that the

---

[1] "Replies to Canright," p. 112.

religious world will be divided into just two classes, those who keep the Sabbath and those who oppose it." This explains their zeal in proselyting. These 144,000 Adventists will be privileged in heaven above all others as the special body-guard of Christ through all eternity. Of them the "History of the Sabbath," edition 1912, page 812 says: "They will be the special body-guard of the Lamb!" Mrs. White says: "The living saints, 144,000 in number, heard the day and hour of Jesus coming."[1] Of the most glorious place in heaven Jesus said, "Only the 144,000 enter this place" (page 14). There "the names of the 144,000 were engraved in letters of gold" (page 15). Again: The angel said to her, "If you are faithful, you, with the 144,000, shall have the privilege of visiting all the worlds and viewing the handiworks of God" (page 33). These Adventists are to spend eternity in pleasure trips to "all the worlds"! They are to be a very select company all because they kept Saturday instead of Sunday! The prophets, apostles, and martyrs will not be in it with them! As to the reasonableness of such celestial pleasure trips the reader may judge.

In "Great Controversy," edition of 1884, Mrs. White devotes six chapters, 31 to 37, or 94 pages, describing ahead in detail the awful things to occur just before the end. The Holy Ghost will baptize the Adventists as on Pentecost. They will go everywhere with a "loud cry," work miracles, per-

[1] "Early Writings," edition of 1882, p. 11.

form wonders, show signs, and every true Christian on all the earth will "come out of Babylon" and join them. Then Satan will come personally in great glory, walk among men, talk with them familiarly, go all around the earth that way. He claims to be Christ himself and is accepted as such by all Churches and statesmen. He now says that Sunday is his holy day and urges that all Adventists must be killed for preaching against it. His advice is accepted and a decree of death against them is passed in every nation of earth. Just then Jesus comes, and delivers them. This is all to occur right off, possibly in a year or two, soon anyway. Since the beginning of the world no such thing as this has been seen. There is no scripture for it. It rests solely on the word of Mrs. White, yet they all believe it, and are hurrying to be ready for it by disposing of their property, etc. It borders close on to fanaticism and must end in a catastrophe.

THEIR EXTREME VIEWS ON DIET

The following quotations from Mrs. White's "Testimonies to the Church" give an idea of their extreme views on diet. Remember that these are accepted as divine commandments to be expressly obeyed. The following quotations are from Volume II, page 61: "You have used the fat of animals which God in His word expressly forbids." Page 68: "Cheese should never be introduced into the stomach." Page 70: "It is just as much sin

ADVENTISM, WHAT IS IT? 51

to violate the laws of our being as to break one of the Ten Commandments." Page 96: "The use of swine's flesh is contrary to His express commandments." Page 400: "Eggs should not be placed upon your table. They are an injury to your children." Volume III, page 21: "We bear a positive testimony against tobacco, spirituous liquors, snuff, tea, coffee, flesh meats, butter, spices, rich cake, mince pies, a large amount of sugar and all sweet substances used as articles of food."

Well, then, what are we permitted to eat? Here it is—Volume II, page 67: "A plain simple diet, composed of unbolted wheat flour, vegetables, victuals prepared without spices or grease." Notice it is just as big a sin to eat a piece of pork as it is to break one of the commandments, which forbids lying, adultery, stealing, etc.! Notice further that the whole tendency of this system is to go back to the laws of the Old Testament, which were designed for a local people in a limited territory and for a limited time. When the Gospel was to go to all the world, these laws could not be applied. Think of missionaries among the Eskimos in the winter, trying to live on this diet! The directions in the New Testament are directly contrary to Mrs. White's revelations. Jesus said, Luke x. 8: "And into whatsoever city ye enter and they receive you, eat such things as are set before you." And Paul said the same, 1 Cor. x. 25: "Whatsoever is sold in the shambles (meat market) that eat asking no question for conscience sake." And

Romans xiv. 17: "For the kingdom of God is not meat and drink, but righteousness and peace and joy in the Holy Ghost." These texts, and many more, strongly contradict the rigid rules laid down by Adventists.

THE HARM IT DOES

1. It imposes on conscientious people an unnecessary sacrifice not required by the Gospel.
2. Its advocates become very annoying to other Christian workers as devoted as themselves.
3. Their work largely is to divide or break up other Churches and missions wherever they can.
4. It creates an unnecessary division and confusion in neighborhoods otherwise united in a day of rest.
5. It sows distrust of all other Churches in the minds of thousands who do not join the Adventists, neither can they be reached by other Churches after that.
6. A large share of their children give up the Sabbath as soon as they are grown. Then they keep neither Saturday nor Sunday, nor attend any church, but drift to perdition. There are thousands of these now scattered everywhere.
7. As their meetings are held on Saturday, no one attends but their own people. If left to them, the mass of any community could never hear the Gospel.
8. The evangelical Churches hold all the Gospel truth Adventists have, but without their errors.

9. By staking all on a certain limited time, as they have done in the past, and are now doing again, limiting it to the generation beginning in 1844, the passing of their set limits, ends them in disaster, as this must do in time.

Their power lies in their unbounded faith in their "message," not in any truth they teach. Evident sincerity, clean lives, great zeal and positive assertions win people regardless of whether or not their doctrines are reasonable and Scriptural. Christian Science, in many respects, is exactly the opposite of Adventism, and yet it spreads several times as fast. So does Catholicism and other isms.

This brief sketch will give the reader a fair idea of what Seventh-Day Adventism is, and what it hopes to accomplish. It is hoped that the following chapters will help to save honest persons from falling into that error.

II

THE "RELIGIOUS LIBERTY" SCARECROW

AS early as 1847, in their very first printed publication, "A Word to the Little Flock," published at Brunswick, Maine, May 30, 1846, Elder White argued from Rev. xiii. 11-18, that just before Jesus appears, a decree must go forth to kill the saints.[1] In this pamphlet, page 19, Mrs. White records a vision in which she says "the wicked took council to rid the earth of us. We all fled from the cities and villages, but were pursued by the wicked who entered the houses of the saints with the sword. They raised the sword to kill us, but it broke, and fell as powerless as a straw."

From that day till this, Seventh-Day Adventists have continued predicting that this persecution would come upon them. Why were they to be thus outlawed? Simply because they would not refrain from work on Sunday, " The Pope's Day." What power is to pass this death decree? It was to be the United States, represented by the lamb-like beast of Rev. xiii. 11-18. So Adventists said. In my other book, pages 85 to 116, it is clearly proved that this symbol cannot possibly apply to

[1] "A Word to the Little Flock," p. 10.

our nation. That beast kills the saints (Rev. xiii. 15; xx. 4). But the Adventists say that not one of them will be killed. This would contradict that prophecy, if it applies to them.

So long as their work was confined to the United States, Adventists limited that decree of death to this nation. But recently, since their work has extended to all nations, they have also extended that prophecy to all the world. Now a stringent, Puritan Sunday law is to be decreed by every nation on earth with that death penalty for a disregard of that day! The *Advent Review* of January 7, 1915, has a lengthy editorial, arguing that there will be a world-wide confederacy of all nations with the President of the United States as the head of it!

Then that world-wide power will pass the long expected Sunday law with the death penalty in every nation on earth. I will quote a few sentences:

"What is more natural than that such a confederation should declare for a Sunday Sabbath obligatory upon *all the people of the world?* Some President will take the step [to issue that decree] when the time is ripe. The United States, according to the prophecy, is to lead the world in bringing to a head that movement which must culminate in the universal decree which demands the worship of the beast [keeping Sunday] on the *pain of death.*" The *Advent Review*, February 4, 1915, says: "By means of the Sunday Sabbath the 'man of sin' will cause *all the world to worship him as God.*

According to the prophecy of Revelation xiii., as far as the majority are concerned, he will succeed in his deception."

This is only a sample of what Adventists are constantly predicting. Mrs. White's latest revelations are urging with vehement appeals to her followers that this event is right upon them. They must *hurry, hurry, hurry,* and "finish the work" before the decree goes forth and their goods are all confiscated and they are all sentenced to death! If any wild brain ever imagined a theory more improbable than this I never read of it. The President of the United States is to become the head of all the nations of the world in one Universal Confederacy. This would include England, France, Germany, Austria, Italy, Russia, Turkey, China, Japan, and all the republics of South America! Then he will influence all these various nations to enact a strict Sunday law with the death penalty, for a desecration of the day! Consider this fact: The population of the globe to-day is sixteen hundred million. Of these there are four hundred million Chinese who keep no day of the week, but work Sunday the same as on other days. Then the Mohammedans, two hundred million, have their Sabbath on Friday and work Sunday; India, with three hundred and fifteen million, has no weekly rest day. Then comes Japan, Korea, all the millions of Africa, who have no regard for Sunday.

Out of the sixteen hundred million on earth, ten

hundred million (almost two-thirds) have never had any regard for Sunday and do not now. They are opposed to Christianity. Can all these suddenly be brought to keep Sunday themselves so strictly that all these nations will join in a Sunday law so strict that it will be death to disregard it? And all this is to happen right off—perhaps in five years!

Then, of professing Christians, two hundred and fifty million are Roman Catholic, as in Spain, Portugal, Italy, Austria, France, Mexico, and all the South American States. These Catholics are notoriously loose in Sunday observance, and ridicule the Protestant idea of Sunday sacredness. Thus, the *Ecclesiastical Review*, February, 1914 (a standard Catholic monthly), page 250, says: "Protestants make much of the observance of the Sunday and are sometimes sincerely and honestly shocked that we Catholics seem to make little of that same observance." They attend mass forenoon, then attend ball-games, beer-gardens, bull-fights, dances, elections, or work if they choose. Contrary to all their theories and practices for ages past, are all these to suddenly turn square about and observe Sunday so strictly as to enact a law with the penalty of death for desecrating that day? Then there are one hundred and fifty million Greek Catholics comprising nearly all the vast Russian empire, the Balkan states, etc. These regard Sunday as loosely as Roman Catholics. With many of them Sunday is a market-day after a morning service.

Then a large share of Protestants pay only a slight regard to the observance of Sunday. They go on excursions, auto-riding, fishing, ball-games, and large numbers work on the street cars, railroads, boats, in their gardens, on their farms, and in many other ways.

Then take the non-churchgoing people comprising more than half the population in all Christian lands. Largely, they pay only a loose regard to Sunday. Every observing man must see that the whole trend in all lands is directly the opposite of a stricter Sunday observance.

In the face of all this, Adventists expect the whole world—heathen, Mohammedan, Roman Catholic, Greek, worldlings, socialists, saloon-men, infidels,—all to suddenly turn around and unite to enact a world-wide Sunday law with a death penalty! All this is to come quickly, possibly in less than five years. Have these brethren lost their reason, their common sense? Such a radical, world-wide revolution in so short a time would be contrary to all the history of the past. All natural causes and the general growth of new ideas must be ignored and an unheard-of miracle must be assumed, to fulfill their predictions. It smacks strongly of fanaticism.

Instead of a spirit of intolerance and religious persecution growing in the world, the whole trend is all the other way, not only in America, but the world over. Freedom of thought, freedom of speech, freedom of the press, freedom of religious and political views are coming more and more to be respected. Persecution for religious views is growing to be more unpopular, and less and less practiced. The rack, the inquisition, torture, burning at the stake, hanging, etc., all too common centuries ago, would not now be tolerated in any civilized country. Even despotic Russia, Austria and Spain have outgrown these. The death penalty, even for murder, is coming largely to be condemned. Will this, our free and enlightened nation, soon issue an edict to slaughter a whole denomination of honest people simply for believing that Sunday is not a holy day? Will they then all be condemned to be killed, men, women, children, simply for an opinion? Can an intelligent man believe that?

The effort in some states to close the manufacturing plants, shut up barber shops, close the saloon, and restrict work on Sunday, is largely in the interest of laboring men, and is being demanded by them that they may have a day of rest and leisure with their families, as well as the wealthy class. It is simply along the general trend of human progress to secure better conditions for the overworked, toiling men, women and children. This is seen in the effort to limit the ages under which children cannot be employed in factories; the number of hours beyond which women cannot be employed in each week; the closing of stores at 6 P. M. instead of working the clerks to late hours; the Saturday half-holiday; and the nine hour, even now the eight hour, working-day. Sunday-closing is along the same line, and largely for the same purpose, and is being demanded by working-people, many of whom care little for religion and less for the Church.

Of course Christian people favor it, as it secures to them the privilege of religious service. If all business was free to operate on Sunday, thousands of Christians would be compelled, against their conscience, to work that day to keep their jobs and support their families. Hence, the majority of intelligent people, worldlings and Christians, are united in wishing a Sunday rest-day for the betterment of society in general. In this there is no thought of persecuting Adventists. Most of the states already have Sunday laws forbidding general work on that day; yet Adventists go right on with their work freely. Where, in a few cases, some have been arrested out of spite, popular sentiment of judges and juries has been opposed to it and only a nominal fine, or none at all, has been made except in rare cases years ago, but none of late.

Take the world over during the seventy years Adventists have been predicting a religious persecution, and the laws, in all nations, have gone just the other way. Seventy years ago Christian missionaries were either entirely shut out of a large part of the heathen and Mohammedan countries, or had to work under the most oppressive restrictions. Protestants, also, were so persecuted and hampered in such countries as Russia, Austria, Spain, Mexico and all the Catholic countries of South America, that they could do little. But steadily, through these seventy years, the oppressive laws have been modified and all these countries are now open to the Gospel nearly, or quite, as freely as at home. Adventists themselves now have missions in nearly every nation on earth and are seldom molested. Even twenty-five years ago they could not have done this. All this contradicts what they have predicted and are still preaching " None so blind as those who will not see."

February 27, 1915, Bruce McRae, Corresponding Secretary of the Actors' Association of New York, reported as follows:

" This association, representing over two thousand of the most representative actors and actresses, desires to go on record,—that inasmuch as the legalizing of Sunday performances would be a great injustice to the members of the theatrical profession, it would oppose it with all the influence that it could command.

" The actor needs his Sunday's rest as does any other brain worker and when his position is sufficiently influential, he gets it." [1]

Thousands of actors complain that their managers, when a Sunday law does not prohibit it, compel them to work seven days for six days' pay, and that such continuous work breaks them down. Adventists oppose all efforts to relieve these and hun-

[1] In the Bulletin of the New York Sabbath Committee, April, 1915.

dreds of thousands of other overworked toilers. Their opposition is supremely selfish, born of a misguided zeal.

In many states Barbers' Associations are demanding the same as the actors for the same reason. Religious worship is not the idea of any of their associations. What they want is simply to have the privilege of a day of rest like other people.

In closing work on Sunday there is no thought of compelling people to go to church or to be religious. But it is desired by Christians to give people a chance to hear the Gospel if they wish to. We do not close the saloons to compel the men to be sober, but to remove from them the temptation to drink. Hence it is unfair, and untruthful, to argue that Sunday laws are made to compel men to go to church or to become religious.

ADVENTISTS BACK DOWN ON SUNDAY WORK

Recently Mrs. White had a revelation directing her people, the world over, to refrain from work on Sunday whenever the law requires it. They will all readily obey. How, then, can they be persecuted for Sunday work when none of them work that day? In Australia, a law required Adventists to close their publishing houses on Sunday. For three Sundays they did not obey. Then they were threatened with arrest. What now? Did they brave the law and take the penalty as they always said they would? Mrs. White, their divine oracle, fortunately was right there. Did she counsel martyrdom? Oh, no! she immediately produced a revelation directing them to obey the law, close the plant on Sunday and devote the day to the Lord in religious work just as Sunday-keepers do. Here are her instructions in "Testimonies to the Church," Volume IX, Number 37, published in 1909. It is a square back down from all she had published before. It avoids all possibility of persecution for Sunday work. She says, "The light given me by the Lord at a time when we were expecting just such a crisis as you seem to be approaching was that when the people were moved by a power from beneath to enforce Sunday observance, Seventh-Day Adventists were to show their wisdom by refraining from their ordinary work on that day, devoting it to missionary effort." Page 232: "Give them no occasion to call you lawbreakers." "It will be very easy to avoid that difficulty. Give Sunday to the Lord as a day for doing missionary work."

"At one time, those in charge of our school at Avondale [Australia] inquired of me, saying, 'What shall we do? The officers of the law have been commissioned to arrest those working on Sunday.' I replied, 'It will be very easy to avoid that difficulty. Give Sunday to the Lord as a day for doing missionary work. Take the students out to hold meetings in different places, and to do medical missionary work. They will find the people at home, and will have a splendid opportunity to present the truth. *This way of spending Sunday is always acceptable to the Lord*'" (page 238).

It will be readily seen that Mrs. White now directs her people to keep Sunday exactly as all conscientious Sunday observers do; that is, in holding religious meetings and doing religious work! *"They are to refrain from their ordinary work on that day. Give Sunday to the Lord as a day of doing missionary work. This way of spending Sunday is always acceptable to the Lord."*

A prospect of arrest suddenly converted Mrs. White to a zealous religious observance of Sunday. "Give the day to the Lord." And then especially notice: "This way of spending Sunday is always acceptable to the Lord." Good and true. Now if it is acceptable to the Lord from Adventists, it must be acceptable to the Lord from Methodists, Baptists, etc. Why not?

But the point is this: If Adventists follow this advice, how will they be persecuted for working on Sunday? What becomes of the prediction that an edict will be issued to kill them all for violating a Sunday law? That was what Adventists have always taught before. But in 1909 they were directed to observe Sunday strictly and obey the law!

If the prospect of simply a fine will cause Adventists to obey the law and refrain from work on Sunday, would not the prospect of a death penalty quickly induce them to obey? Surely. It shows that their theory breaks down when really tested. Then if Baptists, Methodists, etc., have the mark of the beast because they "give Sunday to the Lord" in religious service, why will not Adventists also have it if they gave the day to the Lord in the same way? Of course they will.

A STRICT SUNDAY LAW WOULD IN NO WAY INTERFERE WITH THE RELIGIOUS LIBERTY OF ADVENTISTS

The Adventists publish a *Liberty Magazine* wholly devoted to an effort to prove that a Sunday law would restrict their religious liberty and require them to violate their conscience. Their position is untenable, their arguments fallacious. It would do no such thing. Mrs. White herself, as above, has proved their contention untrue. How? She directs them to obey the law and do no work on Sunday. Would she advise them to violate their conscience, disobey God? And neglect a sacred duty to avoid a fine? Surely not. Then she does not regard it as a religious duty to work on Sunday, nor do they, or they would not advocate what she directs.

Why does an Adventist work on Sunday? Does he do it as an act of worship? No, he works for money, for the financial gain there is in it. That is all. If an Adventist was receiving two dollars per day for Sunday work, and should be offered four dollars per day to simply remain at home, would he not accept the offer? Yes readily, and why shouldn't he? He violates none of his religious principles. He works to get money, and sits still to get more, that is all. A law forbidding manual labor on Sunday deprives him of no religious privileges. At home he can read his Bible or any religious book; or write articles, or pray; he can go to any church; or to his own; he can hold public meetings and teach his doctrines freely; he can go from house to house with his literature and teach his doctrines there. He is not required to attend church where he does not care to, nor profess any creed he does not believe, nor deny what he does believe. How then would a law prohibiting work on Sunday interfere with his religious liberty? That is only a scarecrow of straw of their own making and that is all.

The saloon-keeper wants to keep his saloon open on Sunday. What for? As a religious duty? To worship God? He does it for gain, for business. He says the law restricts his personal liberty. Theatrical and moving picture proprietors insist on conducting their business on Sunday. Do they do it as a religious duty? No. Neither do Adventists work Sunday as an act of worship, or as a religious duty. It is a business proposition and that is all.

Then every one knows that Saturday is observed the world over by the Adventists as their sacred day for religious worship. Any law which does not interfere with worshipping on Saturday has no bearing whatever upon the religious liberty of Seventh-Day worshippers. But a Sunday closing statute in no way applies to Saturday any more than it does to Friday. There is no complaint coming for Saturday-observing Jews, or Friday-observing Mohammedans that a Sunday law infringes upon their religious liberties. The Adventists will be just as free to worship on the Jewish Sabbath under the most stringent Sunday law as they are now in California, where at present there is no Sunday legislation. And this they know right well. It is illogical and unreasonable, and wholly without excuse, for them to oppose a Sunday law on the ground that it will deprive them of their religious liberties.

ONLY THEIR CIVIL LIBERTY ABRIDGED

All that Adventists can truthfully claim is that a Sunday law would abridge their *civil liberty*—their personal freedom. Here their arguments lie very close along the line of the saloon men and liquor users—*personal liberty*. But any person who chooses to live among other people has to pay for that privilege by giving up many personal rights which he might exercise freely if he lived by himself alone. Suppose a man with a family lived on an island away from all others, as Robinson Crusoe did. He could go naked, go loaded with firearms, get drunk, smoke and spit tobacco-juice anywhere, build his house anywhere, of any kind of material, make all the noise he chooses, let his cattle run loose, let his children go uneducated, hunt or fish all seasons of the year for any kind of game or fish, and do many other things unmolested.

Now let him move into a civilized farming community. He would immediately have to sacrifice all these rights. He could not go naked nor keep his children out of school, nor let his cattle run loose, nor hunt or fish out of season, nor leave a dead animal by the roadside, etc.

When he goes to the city, he must not spit on the sidewalk, nor get drunk, nor beg on the street, nor drive on the left side of the street, nor cross a main street without a signal from the police, nor turn a corner only in such a way, nor drive only so fast, nor leave his team there only so long, nor leave them unblanketed in the cold, nor allow his boy to work in the shop under a certain age, nor his daughter to work in a shop more than so many hours per week, and many more such things.

This is simply what is called "Police Power" delegated to every state, through all its agencies, both general and local, to preserve order, regulate intercourse between citizens, and to insure to each the lawful enjoyment of his rights.

The civil power is the power of arbitrary force to compel men who will not be righteous to at least be civil, that men may live together in peace and quietness. (See Appendix A, page 261.)

In return for the personal restrictions which are necessarily placed on each member of society, this protects his property, his person, and his personal freedom as far as consistent with the rights of others and the general good of society. Polygamy is a religious tenet of the Utah Mormons which they hold as strongly as Adventists hold the Sabbath. Here the law has restricted their "religious liberty." Would Adventists leave them free, anywhere and everywhere, with their many wives? In India, mothers threw their children into the river as a religious duty, and wives were burned alive with husbands when they died. British law stopped this "religious freedom." What do Adventists say to that?

All this is the price a person must pay for the privilege of being a citizen with other fellow citizens whose rights and conveniences must be consulted as well as his own. This is a universal law, recognized among all civilized people. Without it, we would have lawlessness and anarchy. What is for the best interests of the whole must be considered, not simply the convenience of the few. This is democracy and is just and right. It is the word of God too. Paul says: "For none of us liveth to himself" (Rom. xiv. 7). "Look not every man on his own things but every man also on the things of others" (Phil. ii. 4). "Thou shalt love thy neighbor as thyself" (Mark xii. 31). A Christian will sacrifice much rather than annoy his neighbor. The one, the few, the minority, must harmonize with the majority as far as they can without sacrificing principles. An Adventist sacrifices no moral or religious principle when he abstains from manual work on Sunday. He foregoes a business gain for the general wish and social good of the majority. If the law required Adventists *to work on Saturday*, that would be a different thing. That would require them to violate their conscience and break the law of God as they believe. But no such thing is proposed or thought of.

Besides, there is a growing tendency on the part of our state legislatures to exempt in the Sunday laws, all who observe some other day as a day of worship and who refrain from business and labor on that day, from the Sunday prohibitions. But, strange to say, Adventists oppose these exemptions made for their protection as much as any other part of the Sunday bill. It is a proof that they are not sincere in grounding their opposition to Sunday legislation upon the protection of their civil and religious rights. Many of the states have already adopted such exemption clauses.

Adventists should be the first to recognize the great value of a rest day each week for all men. To them, resting on the Sabbath once a week is the most important of all duties. If a weekly Sabbath is of so much benefit to them, then it will be so to all others and they should aid them to secure such a weekly rest day. But they cannot, and do not, expect to win the majority over to give up Sunday and keep Saturday instead. A few in each community is all they have ever succeeded in getting. Do they wish all the rest of the great majority to have no Sabbath? Their whole effort and influence is that way—to have a Sabbathless and churchless community. They confuse thousands of people who, after that, keep no day. They argue that every Sunday law is unconstitutional. They bitterly oppose any and every Sunday restriction.

They argue that all business should continue on Sunday the same as on any week day. They would have saloons open on Sunday the same as on Monday. They all work themselves Sunday and ridicule Sunday keepers as pagans and papists. If their influence prevailed, society would soon be demoralized. Adventists strongly oppose three of the greatest bulwarks of our government, namely: the public school, the churches, and a Sunday rest-day.

Consider a moment: Sunday is just as long as Saturday—to a minute. It affords every advantage that Saturday does, physical rest, mental rest, social privileges, time for reading the Bible and religious work, prayers, attendance at church and Bible school, song service, etc. There is no difference in the advantages of the one day over the other, so far as the use of the day is concerned. But Sunday has the great advantage of being the day on which the people generally rest and so the day is quiet. Moreover, the vast majority of those who observe Sunday conscientiously suppose they are keeping the day in obedience to the Lord's will. They keep it as "the Sabbath" just the same as Adventists keep Saturday.

Their motive is to serve God. They have not the remotest idea of reverencing the Papacy, or the sun, or paganism. As God looks at the heart, at the motive, does He not accept such sincere service? Paul says they that "regard the day unto the Lord" (Rom. xiv. 6) are acceptable to God. Adventists do no more than this in keeping Saturday.

In keeping Sunday we preserve the model of the seven days of creation, and thus are reminded of the creation as plainly as Adventists are. Added to this we also commemorate the resurrection, the key-note of the entire Gospel. Here the Jewish Sabbath fails to remind us of anything in the Gospel. For twenty-eight years I myself kept conscientiously the seventh day unto the Lord. Now, for twenty-eight years, I have kept Sunday unto the Lord. The first was dry duty,—bondage: the last is privilege—liberty, and I like it the best.

SEVENTH DAY ADVENTISTS USE POLITICAL METHODS WHICH THEY CONDEMN IN ALL OTHERS

Adventists condemn in strong terms the efforts of Catholics and the Federation of Churches to influence legislatures and legislation in their favor. They are constantly denouncing both these religious bodies for trying to influence men in office to secure the law they wish, or to defeat laws they do not favor. They condemn this as using worldly and unchristian methods to further religious views. But, strange to say, Adventists do the very same thing themselves and they use every possible means in their power to accomplish it. They keep trained and paid men in every conference to watch every state legislature and congress for any Sunday legislation. These men are furnished with an abundance of specially prepared literature and are on the alert to personally influence every man in office from the President down to the mayor and common voters. They boast that they have defeated many a Sunday bill in Congress and in the states.

They publish a *Liberty Magazine* for this express purpose. In proof read the following: "Elder E. L. Cardey, religious liberty secretary of the Greater New York conference, writes that the executive committee has voted to send the current number of *Liberty* to 500 judges and attorneys in that conference."

"The District of Columbia conference has decided to unite with the North American Division Religious Liberty Department in circulating 900 copies of *Liberty* each quarter among the United States senators, representatives, and other moulders of public opinion at the Capital of our nation. If you wish to help in this good work, it will cost you only $1.00 to send *Liberty* to five of these persons of influence for one year. Send the order to your tract society. We will furnish the names of legislators, public-school teachers, attorneys, judges, as you may prefer. Send this issue of *Liberty* to all lawyers and judges of our conference." [1]

This gives a fair idea of what they are trying to do. Every member of every church is urged to do his utmost along this line, and largely he does it. No Protestant Church, not even Catholics, work as zealously along this line as Adventists do. And they have the most efficient organization in the world to carry it out. It shows what they will do, if they ever become numerous enough to have political influence.

[1] *Adventist Review*, Jan. 14, 1915.

III

ADVENTISTS ASSERT THAT THE CATHOLIC CHURCH CHANGED THE SABBATH; BUT WHICH CATHOLIC CHURCH?

ADVENTISTS repeat this assertion, in various ways, so constantly that their people believe it to be absolutely true. Their children are taught this as thoroughly as they are the Bible. Any one at all familiar with their teachings needs no proof that they make the above claim.

Mrs. White says: "The Pope had changed it [the Sabbath] from the seventh to the first day of the week."[1] The following is from the *Signs of Times Magazine*, October, 1914:

"Sunday is the first day of the week and its observance belongs to the Catholic Church."

"Every one who accepts the Sunday institution as a Sabbath thereby accepts an institution of the Catholic Church."

"The Catholic Church says: 'By my divine power I have abolished the Sabbath day and command you to keep the first day of the week! And lo, the entire civilized world bows down in reverent obedience to the command of the Holy Catholic Church.'"

[1] "Early Writings," p. 26.

But there are two damaging objections to this theory.

First: Adventists assume and argue on the assumption that the "Catholic Church" began to be formed about three hundred years after Christ. Hence, if the Catholic Church did change the Sabbath, the change could not have been made before that late date. Then they easily find, and gladly quote, a large number of Catholic catechisms, Catholic priests, and Catholic challenges to Protestants, all boasting that the Holy Catholic Church changed the Sabbath. Adventists say that this settles the question.

Second: But in this they ignore, fail to state, another claim which all these same Catholic authorities always make just as strongly, namely, that their Holy Catholic Church extends back to, and began with, the apostles, and that the change was made by them. If Adventists accept one claim of the Catholics, then, to be fair, they should accept both. But this would overthrow their argument.

Now the simple fact is, the original "Catholic" Church, which did actually begin with the apostles where the day was changed, is not the same Church as the Roman Catholic Church, or the Papacy, of a much later date. The ground on which the Roman Catholic Church makes the false claim that she changed the Sabbath is by making the further false claim that the present Roman Church extends back to, and includes the apostles, who, they readily agree, made the change. Both these facts are abundantly proved by the testimony of Catholics themselves. It is by ignoring these fundamental facts that Adventists can use quotations from Catholics as they do. Their lay members and the common people do not know this, and hence are easily deceived.

No class of people denounces the Roman Church more strongly than Adventists do. They pronounce them deceivers, false teachers, perverters of history, and their boastful claims they repudiate as worthless, all except on the change of the Sabbath. Here they hold up, and publish to the world, her mere assertion as settling the question beyond dispute. The Catholics offer no proof of their claim that they changed the day. They *assert* that they did and leave it there. Adventists gladly accept this without any proof. Consider now: The Roman Catholic Church makes all the following boastful claims:

1. The Roman Catholic Church is the only true Church.
2. St. Peter was the first Pope of the Holy Catholic Church.
3. The present Pope of Rome is the lineal divinely appointed successor of St. Peter.
4. The Pope of Rome is the Vicar of Jesus Christ upon earth.
5. The Pope is infallible.
6. The Pope holds the keys to heaven.
7. All, including Adventists, outside of the Catholic Church are heretics.

8. Protestants are indebted to Catholics for the Holy Scriptures as it is given to them.

9. Catholic priests have authority to forgive sins.

10. The Roman Catholic Church changed the Sabbath from the seventh day to Sunday, the first day.

The Catholic Church strongly claims all these ten items. What do Seventh-Day Adventists say to these assertions? They quickly deny all the first nine, say they are all lies, without any foundation in fact. But when you come to the tenth one, the change of the Sabbath, then Adventists fall over each other to accept every word of this as the infallible truth. It settles the question beyond dispute. "The Catholic Church just owns it right up" that it did really do the job!!

To illustrate: Adventists bring their chief witness into court. But when he is sworn they acknowledge that nine-tenths of his testimony is a lie, is perjury, but one-tenth of what he swears to is true. On this they claim they have won their case! Sela!

Any judge would quickly throw out of court such testimony as worthless, yet this is the witness, and the only witness, Adventists can produce saying that the Roman Church changed the Sabbath. See any of their publications on this point.

We will now examine this witness.

The Roman Catholic Church claims to extend back to the apostles and include them. This is so well known that no proof need be offered. Yet I will give a few quotations. Cardinal Gibbons is the highest Catholic authority in America. His work of 480 pages, "The Faith of Our Fathers," is written expressly to prove that the modern Roman Catholic Church dates back to Christ and the apostles and has continued in an unbroken succession down to the present time. He claims that St. Peter was the first Pope and that his office and authority have descended unbroken through all the Popes to the present one. On page 58 he says: "The true Church must be Apostolical. Her ministers must derive their power from the apostles by an unbroken succession." On page 67 he gives a table of the true Church, the Catholic, thus:

| Name of Sect | Place of Origin | Founder | Year | Authority |
| Catholic Church | Jerusalem | Jesus Christ | 33 | New Testament |

On pages 68 and 69 he says all the Protestant sects "came fifteen hundred years too late to have any pretensions to be called the Apostolic Church." "The Catholic Church, on the contrary, can easily vindicate the title of Apostolic, because she derives her origin from the Apostles." "Thus we go back from century to century till we come to Peter, the first Bishop of Rome, Prince of the Apostles, and Vicar of Christ." On page 87 he says: "She is the only Church which is acknowledged to have existed from the beginning." Again, page 167, "St. Peter, the first Pope in the long, unbroken line of Sovereign Pontiffs."

WHICH CATHOLIC CHURCH? 79

The "Catholic Dictionary," Article "Catholic Church," says: "General or universal. It was applied to the true Church spread throughout the world." "The present Catholic Roman Church is the Church founded by Christ."

I have just examined a large number of Catholic works from the smallest catechism up to their great "Encyclopedia," and all agree in contending that the Catholic Church goes back to the apostles and includes them with Peter as the first Pope. On this assumption they found the claim that whatever was done by the apostles was done by the Roman Catholic Church. *Mark this fact well*, for on this claim rests the assertion of Catholics that their Church changed the Sabbath.

The Pope. The name, "Pope," simply means father. For centuries after Christ that was the common name for all priests, both in the Roman and Greek Church. It meant then the same as "pastor" now means with us. Later, in the West, it was gradually restricted to bishops only. In 1073, Gregory VII, in a council, prohibited the use of the title by any one except the Bishop of Rome. So, then, the "Pope," as that term is now used, did not exist till hundreds of years after the time fixed by Adventists for the change of the Sabbath. So it could not have been changed by the "Pope."

The term, "The Catholic Church," is now commonly used to mean the Church of Rome only, with the Pope at its head, and it is now claimed by that Church as belonging exclusively to itself, excluding all others from that name. The Roman Church also claims this title exclusively clear back to the apostles, including them as the founders of their "Catholic Church" with Peter as their first Pope. But this claim is wholly unfounded and contrary to the plainest facts of history. The "Catholic Church" is one thing, the "Roman Church" another thing, and the "Papacy" is still another thing, each differing from the other.

"Catholic" means general, or universal. Beginning with the apostles, or soon after, this was used by Christians the world over to distinguish the Christian Church from the Jewish Church, which was national and local. Later, when heresies came up, "Catholic" meant all orthodox believers everywhere, but excluded the heretics. This continued for over 1,000 years till the final split between the Eastern and Western Churches, A. D. 1052. Then the Eastern Church assumed the title of "The Greek Oriental Orthodox Catholic Church," while the Western Church still continued to use the common name "Catholic." The "New International Dictionary" says: "Catholic: 1. Universal or general; of, or pertaining to the Church universal, designating or pertaining to, the ancient, undivided Church, or a Church or Churches historically continuous with and claiming to be a true representation of it, hence, of the true Apostolic Church; orthodox. The term Catholic originally designated the whole body of Christian believers, was officially appropriated as a title by the Western

Church at the time of its separation from the Eastern Church [1052], which assumed the title of Orthodox. After the Reformation, the Church of Rome, or Roman Catholic Church, asserted its exclusive right to the title and although this right has not been recognized by the Reformed Churches, specially that of the Anglican communion, in practice the title is often so restricted."

This is the truth exactly as to the historical use of the term "Catholic Church." It began with the Apostolic Church and was used by the undivided, or whole Church, during all the early centuries for over a thousand years.

I have before me a book entitled, "Catholic Principles," by Rev. J. W. Westcott, Episcopalian. In this he gives abundant historical proof showing that the term, "Catholic Church," began with the apostles, or immediately after, and embraced all true Christians of orthodox faith in all the world. It continued to be so used till the eleventh century when the Eastern, or Greek Church, separated from the Western, or Roman Church, in A. D. 1052. Then Rome assumed to itself the term Catholic, contrary to its former use through the first eleven centuries. Mr. Westcott says: "To start with, we must be careful not to be misled by the use of names, phrases, and expressions, which meant one thing in the third and fourth centuries and mean quite a different thing in the mouths of modern Roman Catholics in the present century" (page 206). "When Protestants use the word Catholic, they generally refer to the Roman Catholic Church; and it is often a matter of great surprise to them to find that a hundred million of men claim to be Catholics, who are not *Roman* Catholics at all" (page 55). Again, he says, and correctly too: "The quotations we have now given from the early Christian writers prove beyond question that both in name and theory the Christian Church was Catholic from the very first Apostolic days" (page 65).

Thus Johnson's "New Universal Cyclopedia," Article "Catholic Church": "The phrase, Catholic Church, is equivalent to 'universal Church,' and cannot properly be limited to any particular sect or body. It was once employed to distinguish the Christian Church from the Jewish, the latter being restricted to a single nation, while the former was intended for the world."

Hence we must remember that the "Catholic Church" for over ten hundred years included all orthodox, or evangelical, Christians the world over. The great Eastern, or Greek Church, which was founded by the apostles, and was never ruled over by the Roman Church, was the first and by far the largest part of the Catholic, or universal, Church. It bore that title before the Roman Catholic Papacy existed. Hence, it is true that the Catholic Church was founded by Christ and the apostles; but this was very different from the Roman Church or Papacy of centuries later. Hence, when correctly understood, we have no objection to saying that the Sabbath was changed by the "*Catholic Church*," for the change was made by the apostles, the founders of the "Catholic," or universal Church.

Rome is not the "Mother Church." That title belongs to the great Eastern Greek Catholic Church, founded by the apostles long before the Roman Catholic Church existed. That Church now numbers one hundred and fifty millions and is the original "Catholic Church." She was the "Mother Church," and the Roman Church for three hundred years was only a mission church, founded and supported by the Eastern Greek Church. This fact is abundantly supported by history.

Thus Right Rev. Bishop Raphael, of Brooklyn, N. Y., Bishop of the Eastern Greek Church, writes me, March 30, 1914:

"The official name of our Church is 'The Holy Orthodox Catholic Apostolic Church.' It was founded in the time of the apostles and by the twelve apostles, Jesus Christ Himself being the chief corner-stone. Beginning on the day of Pentecost (Acts ii.) our Church has never been subject to the Roman Church, or to the Latin Popes, or to the Papacy. The Roman Church herself was a Greek Mission for nearly 300 years, and the Greek language was the tongue in which the Liturgy, or Mass, was said in the city of Rome. The Church of the East has never from the first been known by any other name than Catholic, nor has she set aside this title in any official document.

It is her inalienable property as the mother Church of Christendom."

The Catholic Church was founded in the East by the apostles thirty years before Paul visited Rome. Pentecost was A. D. 33, and Paul did not visit Rome till A. D. 65. Compare dates in Acts ii. and xxviii. margin. Hence, the original "Catholic Apostolic Church" was not the Roman Church at all, but the Greek Church in the early days of the apostles. All the apostles preached in Greek and all the New Testament, except Matthew, was written in Greek—not a book in Latin. Most of the books were written before Paul or Peter visited Rome. See Acts, etc., for dates. Roman Catholic authorities all locate the change of the Sabbath back with the early work of the apostles. This the following chapter will show. If they themselves are correct on this, as they surely are, then the change of the day was not made by the Roman Church at all, but by the Eastern Mother Catholic Church, before any apostle visited Rome. "Rome's challenge" that she changed the Sabbath is founded on the false assumption that the Roman Catholic Church is the original mother Catholic Church, which is utterly false. It is by hiding this plain historical fact that both Rome and Adventists can join hands in their "Challenge" to Protestant Sunday keepers.

Notice now how Adventists place the origin of the Catholic Church at Rome. "The History of the Sabbath," 1912, says: "The so-called Catholic

Church, true to its Roman origin" (page 449). But did the Catholic Church have its origin at Rome? No indeed. It originated in Jerusalem on Pentecost long before there was any Roman Church. Another Seventh-Day Adventist work says: "The Catholic Church was a growth—a growth of error. —It became Catholic only by lowering the standard of faith and morality so as to admit the heathen."[1]

This statement is not true. The Christian Church was everywhere called the "Catholic" Church from its earliest days in its purest period, centuries before the Roman Papacy existed. Adventists contradict all history by such statements.

But a Seventh-Day Baptist has the candor to admit the facts as they are. Rev. A. H. Lewis, D. D., in "Sabbath and Sunday," says: "In the changes of the first four centuries after Christ, the Eastern Church, which was really the mother Church, and the home of primitive Christianity, was left unaffected by the influences which started the strong current of empire westward by way of Rome" (Chap. XIX, p. 220).

Thus Harnack says: "The Roman Catholic Church afterwards claimed as her own those writers of the first century (60-161)."[2]

But not one of these Christian writers and early Fathers of the first century belonged to the Roman, Latin, or Western Church. All were Greeks, belonging to the Eastern Catholic Church.

---

[1] "Fathers of the Catholic Church," Chap. xviii, p. 329.
[2] "History of Dogma," Vol. III, Chap. iii, p. 213.

So, then, the historical facts are these: The original Catholic Church began with the apostles, and included all Orthodox Christians centuries before the corrupt Roman Catholic Church came up. This later Papal Church had nothing whatever to do with changing the Sabbath. The false claim that the Roman Church changed the day is based on the further false claim by Romanists that she is the original pure apostolical Catholic Church. Intelligent Adventist ministers know this very well, and are not guiltless in omitting to state it. Generally, however, their members are entirely ignorant of these facts. They ignorantly suppose that the Roman Catholic Church is the only Catholic Church.

IV

CATHOLICS LOCATE THE CHANGE OF THE SABBATH BACK WITH THE APOSTLES

THE above is the universally accepted doctrine of the Roman Catholic Church. It is so taught in all her doctrinal works. I have examined a large number of her catechisms, her religious dictionary, her great "Encyclopedia," many of her doctrinal works, and I have interviewed one of her bishops and several of her priests, and find all agreeing in teaching this: The Sabbath was changed by the apostles. Notice carefully: We are not now inquiring as to whether the apostles did really change the Sabbath, but as to what the Catholic Church does believe and teach on this question. In my other book, noticed in first page of this book, it is clearly proved that the change in the day was made in the days of the apostles, hence here I do not go over that ground again. Adventists deny that the apostles had anything to do in changing the day, and confidently quote Catholics in such a way as to give the impression that these Catholic authorities say that their Roman Church, or the Pope, or the Papacy, hundreds of years after Christ, made the change. This is unfair. And then they studiously omit an important part of what Catholics plainly teach, and then construe the other part to mean what Catholics neither believe nor teach. I am very sorry to have to say this, but I wish Adventists might see the wrong of it and tell the whole truth.

We will begin with the very highest authority in the Catholic Church—the Council of Trent. "The Catechism of the Council of Trent," published by order of Pius IV, contains the creed of the Church. Every member has to swear to this creed when he joins the Church, hence it is authoritative. It devotes eight pages to the Sabbath question. It says: "The Sabbath was kept holy from the time of the liberation of the people of Israel from the bondage of Pharaoh; the obligation was to cease with the abrogation of the Jewish worship, of which it formed a part; and it therefore was no longer obligatory after the death of Christ. . . . The apostles therefore resolved to consecrate the first day of the week to the divine worship, and called it 'the Lord's Day'; St. John, in the Apocalypse, makes mention of 'the Lord's Day'; and the apostle commands collection to be made 'on the first day of the week,' that is, according to the interpretation of St. Chrysostom, on the Lord's Day; and thus we are given to understand that even then the Lord's Day was kept holy in the Church" (pages 264, 265).

Notice that this creed says the apostles consecrated the day; it was holy, and was called the Lord's Day. The Scriptures are quoted to prove all this. This is the creed of the Roman Church.

Any Catholic priest or writer teaching differently contradicts the sacred creed of his own Church and violates his oath to believe and teach it.

The following is a decisive witness to the position of the Catholic Church as to when the Sabbath was changed and who changed it. It is a comment on Acts xx. 7, in the Catholic Bible itself. Observe how they place the change just where Protestants do and quote the Bible to prove it:

"'And on the first day of the week.' Here St. Chrysostom, with many other interpreters of the Scripture, explain that the Christians, even at this time, must have changed the Sabbath into the first day of the week (the Lord's Day), as all Christians now keep it: This change was undoubtedly made by the authority of the Church: hence the exercise of the power which Christ had given to her; for He is Lord of the Sabbath."

In 1913 Monsignor John Bunyano was the special representative of the Pope in America. Next to the Pope, he was then the highest official authority of that Church in the United States, and what he says is authoritative. "Why Sunday is the First Day" was the title of an article he furnished the *Washington Times,* October 11, 1913. He says: "In the New Law the time for the fulfillment of this [Sabbath] obligation was changed by the apostles from the Sabbath, or the seventh day of the week, to Sunday, or the first day of the week, primarily to commemorate the resurrection of Jesus Christ, who, early in the morning on the first day of the week, arose, glorious and triumphant, from the dead. Hence it is that in Scripture, the first day of the week is called the 'Lord's Day' (Rev. i. 10). It was also on this same day of the week that the Holy Ghost came down upon the apostles, and that the faith and law of Christ was for the first time solemnly published to the world by them."

On this the *Advent Review and Herald*, October 23, 1913, says:

"As we read this article we should not forget that we are reading the deliberate declaration of the highest official in America of that Church which claims to reach back to Apostolic days."

Here, then, by the highest authority deliberately stated, is the teaching of the Roman Catholic Church as to who changed the Sabbath and the time when it was done. It was done by the apostles, in the time of the apostles. All Seventh-Day Adventists certainly know this, for it was published by the editor in their official organ, *The Advent Review*. Now will they cease teaching that the Catholic Church claims to have changed the Sabbath several hundred years after Christ without Apostolic authority? Remember again the question here is not whether the apostles really did make the change, but what does the Catholic Church claim about it? The papal delegate has settled that.

Cardinal Gibbons comes next in authority. I wrote him with regard to when his Church began and when the day was changed. Here is the answer:

Baltimore, Md., July 23, 1896.

REV. D. M. CANRIGHT,

Dear Sir:—In reply to your favor of the 20th inst., to his Eminence the Cardinal, I beg to say:

First. The Catholic Church dates back to the day when our Lord made St. Peter the visible head of the Church, and when St. Peter established, first at Antioch, then at Rome, the seat of his residence and jurisdiction.

In *these days*, and those immediately following, we find traces of the beginning of the custom of the Sunday observance. You may refer to the Christian writers of that period. (Confer Ignatius ad Magnes, 9; Justin Martyr, 1, Apol. 59; Tertul., Apol. 16.) All these writers speak of the Sunday as the Lord's Day; no other more distinct trace has been preserved, and the mention which occurs in the following centuries rests on the fact of a *previous* custom more or less general.

C. T. THOMAS, Sect.

It will be seen that the Cardinal locates the introduction of the Lord's Day at the beginning of the Church with St. Peter.

After the Cardinal, the next highest dignitary in America is Archbishop Ireland. In answer to my question as to *when* the Catholic Church changed the Sabbath, this high prelate answered as follows:

St. Paul, March 2, 1914.

My dear Sir:

In answer to your question I would state that the Jewish Sabbath was simply a positive precept in the Mosaic law and lapsed with that law. The apostles and early Christians instituted the Sunday as a day of special prayer in honor of the great mysteries of the Christian religion, the resurrection and the coming of the Holy Spirit, both occurring on the first day of the week.

Very sincerely,
JOHN IRELAND.

That is clear, positive, and directly to the point.

Here is another high Catholic authority, "The Catholic Encyclopedia on Doctrine," Article, "Sunday": "Sunday was the first day of the week according to the Jewish method of reckoning time, but for the Christians it began to take the place of the Jewish Sabbath in apostolic times as the day set apart for the public solemn worship of God" (Acts xx. 7; 1 Cor. xvi. 2; Rev. i. 10). The same Encyclopedia, Article, "Sabbath," says: "St. Paul enumerates the Sabbath among the Jewish observances which are not obligatory on Christians (Col. ii. 16; Gal. iv. 9-10; Rom. xiv. 5). The Gentile converts held their religious meetings on Sunday (Acts xx. 7; 1 Cor. xvi. 2), and with the disappearance of the Jewish Church, with the Christian Churches the day was exclusively observed as the Lord's Day."

Notice that Catholics quote the same texts as Protestants do to indicate the change. They trace its origin to the New Testament the same as we do and thus claim Scripture authority for it. It will be seen that all these high Catholic authorities

CATHOLICS AGREE WITH PROTESTANTS 93

agree in locating the change in the days of the apostles and by the apostles.

The following is from "The Catholic Dictionary, the Universal Christian Educator, Containing Doctrine of the Church," by Rev. Wm. A. Addis and Thomas Arnold, A. M., both of the Royal University of Ireland. Endorsed by Cardinal Manning and Cardinal McClosky. There could be no better Catholic authority. Now read, Article "Sunday": "The precept of observing the Sabbath was completely abrogated in the Christian Church. In commemoration of Christ's resurrection, the Church observes Sunday. The observance does not rest on any positive law, of which there is no trace. Sunday is of merely ecclesiastical institution, dating however from the time of the apostles. Such is the opinion of St. Thomas. The Scripture given above (Acts xx. 7; 1 Cor. xvi. 2; Rev. i. 10) shows that the observance of Sunday had begun in the apostolic age; but even were Scripture silent, tradition would put the point beyond doubt."

I quote all these to show only one point; viz., the *time* when Catholics claim the change was made by the Church. They all say it was made by the apostles. No other date is given or suggested.

Now read the written testimony of two Catholic priests:

TESTIMONY OF A CATHOLIC PRIEST

"Having lived for years among the Seventh-Day Adventists, I am familiar with their claims that the

Pope of Rome changed the Sabbath from the seventh to the first day of the week. Such assertions are wholly unfounded. Catholics claim no such thing; but maintain that the apostles themselves established the observance of Sunday and that we received it by tradition from them. The councils and Popes afterwards simply confirmed the keeping of the day as received from the apostles.

"JOHN MEILER,
"Rector of St. John's Church, Healdsburg, Cal."

The following statement I drew up, and read to a leading Catholic priest of Grand Rapids, Mich., who readily signed it, as will be seen below:

"The Catholic doctrine of the change of the Sabbath is this: The apostles, by instruction from Jesus Christ, changed the Sabbath from Saturday to Sunday to commemorate the resurrection of Christ and the descent of the Holy Ghost, both of which occurred on Sunday. The change was made by the apostles themselves, and hence by divine authority, at the very beginning of the Church. There are references to this change in Acts xx. 7; 1 Cor. xvi. 1, 2; Rev. i. 10, etc. Yet these texts do not state positively such a change; hence Catholics go to the statements of the early Christian Fathers, where this change by the apostles is confirmed and put beyond doubt. Catholics also rely upon the tradition of the Church which says that the change was made by the apostles. Catholics never teach that the change of the day was made by the Church two or three hundred years after Christ. Such a statement would be contrary to all the facts of history and the traditions of the Church.

"The Holy Catholic Church began with the apostles. St. Peter was the first Pope. Hence, when they say that the Church changed the Sabbath, they mean that it was done by the Church in the days of the apostles. Neither the Church nor the Pope, two or three hundred years after the apostles, had anything whatever to do with changing the Sabbath, for the change had been made ages before. Catholics do not call the first day of the week the Sabbath, for that was Saturday; but they call it Sunday, or the Lord's Day."

This above statement by Rev. D. M. Canright is true and pure Catholic doctrine.—Rev. James C. Pulcher, Pastor of St. James' Church, Grand Rapids, Mich.

See how all these Catholic authorities agree.

Now come to the catechisms which Adventists are so fond of quoting. This is from a "Systematic Study of the Catholic Religion." It is the one used by all students in the Catholic High School in Grand Rapids, Mich. On page 294 I read, "The Church from the time of the apostles has changed the Sabbath into the Lord's Day." In the Advent book, "Who Changed the Sabbath?" page 9, the following is quoted from the "Catholic Christian Instructed."

"Quest. What are the days which the Church commands to be kept holy?

"Ans. 1. The Sunday, or our Lord's Day, which we observe by *apostolic tradition*, instead of the Sabbath."

You see this catechism refers the change of the Sabbath back to the apostles the same as all other Catholic writers do. The Church did this in the time of the apostles, just as all Protestants teach. Here follows another from the same catechism:

"Quest. What warrant have you for keeping the Sunday, preferable to the ancient Sabbath, which was the Saturday?

"Ans. We have for it the authority of the Catholic Church, and *apostolic tradition*."

Here we are again referred right back to the apostles as before.

I will close this testimony of the Catholics with the following from a "Mission Priest." These are priests of the very highest education and influence. Their "mission" is to go from city to city in all the states to their great church centers and give a course of lectures on Catholic doctrines to both Catholics and non-Catholics. They are the best educated and best posted priests in that Church. So what they teach is of the highest character and reliable as expressing Catholic doctrines. I have obtained from my next door neighbor (a Catholic family whose daughter attends the Catholic High School here) the following book: "A Full Course of Instruction in Explanation of the Catechism," by Rev. J. Perry, edited and adapted to the present wants of Colleges, Academies, and Private Families, by a priest of the Mission. It is endorsed by the Archbishop of St. Louis, Mo. Notice that this is the authority studied in families, high schools, colleges, and academies. Is there any better witness? Now read: "Third [Sabbath] commandment. Its obligation transferred from Saturday to Sunday." "What day of the week is the seventh day or Sabbath Day?" "It is Saturday." "Then why do we not keep Saturday holy?" "Because the Church in the apostles' time transferred the obligation from the seventh to the first day of the week." "Why was this done?" "In honor of Jesus Christ, and therefore the first day of the week is called the Lord's Day (Rev. i. 10). It was on the first day of the week (or Sunday) that Christ rose from the dead; that He commissioned His apostles to teach all nations; that He empowered them to forgive sins; that He sent down upon them the Holy Ghost; it was on this day that the apostles began to preach the doctrines of Christ and to establish the Christian religion" (pages 168-169).

Here it will be seen that the Catholics use exactly the same arguments for the change of the day that all Protestants do, and locate the change at the same date, in the time of the apostles and by the apostles.

But do not the catechism and Catholic writers, when controverting Protestants, assert that the "Holy Catholic Church" changed the day? Certainly, but they also claim that the Catholic Church began with the apostles who changed the day. Do not Adventists know this? Yes. Why, then, do they not tell the whole facts in the case? Let them answer.

Consider the high Catholic authorities quoted on this subject—the Council of Trent; the papal delegate, Cardinal Gibbons; Archbishop Ireland; the Catholic Encyclopedia; the Catholic Dictionary; written statements of priests; and the teachings of the catechism. All agree that the change in the day was made by the apostles. Beyond dispute, this establishes the doctrine of the Catholic Church on the origin of the Lord's Day. Not a single Catholic authority can be quoted teaching that the change of the Sabbath was made by the Popes or by the Papacy centuries later. That is purely an invention of Seventh-Day Adventists.

Here, then, is the testimony of two hundred and fifty million Roman Catholics, all agreeing that the observance of Sunday as the Lord's Day originated with the apostles. Now if Adventists quote the Catholics, then let them abide by their testimony.

Now read "Rome's Challenge," "Father Enright's Challenge," and a lot of other Catholic "challenges," which Adventists gleefully gather up and endorse and peddle the world over as unanswerable. Read them very carefully and notice particularly that not one of these Catholic "challenges" ever locates the *time* when the "Catholic Church" made the change. In all these "Challenges" they adroitly leave this point out, and presume on the ignorance of the general public, which supposes that the Catholic Church began centuries after Christ. Then Adventists take advantage of this popular idea of the Catholic Church and locate the change about 300 years after Christ. Such deception is unworthy of Christian teachers.

The position of Protestants on the change of the Sabbath is so well known that no proof need be given. All hold that the change of the day was made in the days of the apostles and by the apostles. Here I do not argue as to whether they are right or not. I simply state what they believe and teach. I could readily name scores of distinct Churches all differing more or less in various doctrines, such as Lutherans, Episcopalians, Baptists, Methodists, Presbyterians, Congregationalists, Disciples, United Brethren, Dutch Reformed, etc., etc., etc. Go ask any of these, " Why do you keep Sunday?" The answer is simple and always the same by all, " Because Christ rose from the dead that day." " When was this change made?" " After the resurrection." " Who made this change?" " The apostles." All answer the same. I could give many quotations by standard writers from all these Churches saying this. But what is the use? Every intelligent person knows this already. The great Eastern Greek Orthodox Church, numbering one hundred and fifty millions, teaches the same thing. Catholics claim just the same as Protestants do that the change of the day was made in the time of the apostles and by the apostles and quote Acts xx. 7; 1 Cor. xvi. 2; Rev.

i. 10 to prove it just as Protestants do. The only difference is that Roman Catholics claim that their Church goes back to the apostles, begins with them and includes them. Hence, when the apostles changed the day it was done by the "Holy Catholic Church." That is the whole of it. This is exactly what all Protestants teach, except that they deny that the apostles were Roman Catholics. Adventists deny it too. So as to when, why, where, and by whom the day was changed Catholics agree exactly with Protestants, and contradict what Adventists quote them to prove. Reader, remember this, and that Adventist bugbear will frighten you no more.

Hastings' "Dictionary of the Bible," Article "Lord's Day," says, "When Jesus uttered the cry, 'It is finished,' the Mosaic dispensation virtually passed away. His Resurrection, Ascension, and Outpouring of the Holy Spirit were successive affirmations of the great fact, and the destruction of the temple made it plain to all but the blindest. But in the meantime nothing is more striking than the tender way in which the apostles and Christians of Jewish birth were weaned from the old religion. The dead leaves of Judaism fell off gradually. They were not rudely torn off by man. The new facts, the new dogmas, the new ordinances first established themselves, and then, little by little, the incompatibility of the old and the new was realized which necessarily issued in the casting off of the old.

"The old things of Judaism were made new in Christianity. This, however, was not accomplished by a deliberate substitution of one ordinance for another; but first the old ordinances were simply antiquated, and their experience matured under the influence of the Holy Spirit, proved that the positive institutions of the new religion more than fulfilled those of the old." "Jesus enunciated the great truths of the Gospel, and left them to germinate and bear fruit through their own inherent power" (Lewis).

V

THE PAGAN ROMANS AND GREEKS HAD NO WEEKLY DAY OF REST, OR FESTIVAL, OR WORSHIP

ONE of the chief arguments which Seventh-Day Adventists make against Sunday observance is this: They say that the pagan nations, especially the Romans, regarded Sunday as a holiday, or festival day: a day of worship of their heathen gods, particularly the sun, on every Sunday,—hence Sun-day. When these pagans professed Christianity they gradually brought into the Church this pagan custom of a Sunday festival day. Then the apostate Roman Church adopted it from these heathens. So now we are keeping a pagan, papal day, hateful to God. Their literature against Sunday-keeping is largely based on this theory as fundamental. Their "History of the Sabbath" is saturated with this argument. It bristles in their tracts, pamphlets, books, and sermons everywhere and all the time. Their children and members believe it as firmly as they believe the Bible. Hence, they abominate Sunday observance and delight in showing contempt for it in every possible way. If they are wrong here the very bottom drops out of their anti-Sunday arguments. Read a few of their assertions. Elder J. H. Waggoner says: "I only take it upon me to fully and clearly show that the Sunday has its origin as a day of regard and observance in paganism and the Papacy." "I shall show that the authority, the name and the sacredness of Sunday are entirely of pagan origin." "Sunday is in every feature a heathen institution."[1] Also "History of the Sabbath," 1912, page 315: "Sunday was indeed the wild solar holiday of all pagan times."

Scores of such statements are found in their works. By these assertions they frighten the common people into giving up Sunday, because they are not able to answer them. All such statements are absolutely untrue as the following evidence will abundantly prove.

I do not accuse the brethren of any intent to deceive in this matter. Till nearly the last years I was with them I myself taught the same thing. This they now quote against me. I did not mean to be untruthful, but, without personal investigation for myself, simply followed our older authors. I know that the other ministers did the same, and their ministers and writers do the same now. Their quotations on this subject in their recent publications easily prove that. It is not intentional dishonesty, but a lack of a candid investigation of historical facts as they really are.

In my city there is a great Public Library, of

[1] "Replies to Canright," pp. 125, 126, 133.

146,000 volumes, containing all up-to-date publications available. Each department has a clerk who will quickly bring any book or article on any subject wanted. Here I have found much contained in these pages. An editorial in a leading daily says:

"One of the outstanding features of modern life is the fact that specialized knowledge is always on tap for inquiring minds. The first fruits of research may be procured at any up-to-date and extensive library, such as the one which Grand Rapids is fortunate enough to possess."

Knowing that our great state and national institutions of learning maintain specialists in every line of knowledge, I decided to apply to them for information on this subject. These learned scholars would have no inducement to be one-sided or unfair. These specialists have every possible means of information at hand and devote a lifetime of study to their particular branch of knowledge. It is their business to furnish to inquirers the results of their research. Hence I drew up a list of questions fully covering every possible phase of this subject, as will be seen. I carefully avoided giving any intimation of my views, or of the use I wished to make of their replies, so as not in any way to influence their answers.

The world renowned British Museum is the highest authority to which I could refer, so I will give this first. I quote my letter to them with their answer to each question one after the other.

Grand Rapids, Mich., Dec. 8, 1914.
British Museum, Department of History,
  London, England.
  Dear Sirs:—For the information of many who are deeply interested in this subject, would you kindly answer briefly the enclosed questions?
                                      D. M. CANRIGHT.

Here is the answer:

Department of Greek and Roman Antiquities,
  British Museum,
    London, W. C., Dec. 24, 1914.
Sir:
  I am commanded by the Assistant Keeper of Greek and Roman Antiquities to reply as follows to your questions on the ancient week:
  Q. 1. Did the pagan Romans and Greeks ever have any regular weekly day of rest from secular work?
  Ans. No.
  Q. 2. Did they have any regular weekly festival day?
  Ans. No.
  Q. 3. Did they have any regular weekly day when they assembled for pagan worship?
  Ans. No.
  Q. 4. Did they have any special day of the week when individuals went to the temples to pray or make offerings?
  Ans. No; both for Greeks and Romans the *month* was the unit and not the week. The Greek calendar varied in different states but the month was generally divided into three periods of ten days. The Romans reckoned from three fixed points in the month, the Kalend or first, the Nones fifth or seventh, the Ides thirteenth or fifteenth. These

subdivisions in themselves *had no religious significance.* Also in the Roman calendars were nundinal, or market days, at periods of eight days, or, as the Romans reckoned, nine. On these days farm work, etc., stopped and citizens flocked into the town markets. To some extent this may be a regular stoppage of secular work; but it *had no religious significance,* except that it was considered an evil omen when the nundinal coincided with other festival days, *e. g.*, the Nones.

The nundinal period seems derived from a blundering reminiscence of a quarter of a lunar period, and there seems no connection with the later seven days' week (see below).

Q. 5. As Sunday was sacred to the Sun, Monday to the Moon, Saturday to Saturn, etc., were those supposed deities worshipped on their own particular days more than on any other days?

Ans. No; the old worship of the gods was disappearing when the seven-day week came about. The significance of the deities' names was *astrological, not religious, e. g.,* if a person were born on Monday, the moon would influence his horoscope, but the moon was never an object of common worship.

Q. 6. When was our week of seven days first introduced into the Roman calendar?

Ans. There are traces in the literature of the late republic (first cent. B. C.) that the Romans used the week of seven days for astrological purposes, in connection with the many Eastern superstitions of the period. It was probably the third century, A. D. before the seven day week came into common use.

Q. 7. From whom did the Romans learn the week of seven days?

Ans. From the Jews, alternately the Assyrians

and Babylonians; the names were probably fixed by the Hellenistic Greeks.

Q. 8. Did the pagan Greeks ever adopt in common life, or in their calendar, the week of seven days?

Ans. No.

Q. 9. Did Apollo, the Sungod, either among the Romans or Greeks, have any special day on which he was worshipped with prayers or offerings more than on any other day?

Ans. There were certain set festivals at various temples; *these were annual, not weekly.*

Q. 10. Did the pagan reverence for Sunday have anything to do in influencing Christians to select that day as their rest day?

Ans. No; it can hardly be said that there was any special reverence for Sunday in pagan times (see answer to No. 5).

I am, sir,
Your obedient servant,
F. N. PRYCE.

You see this historian gives an unqualified NO to all the questions. Notice particularly that the names of the days of the week were all only *astrological*, not religious. There was no religious sacredness attached to a day because it was named after some planet as Sun-day—Sun's day—or Monday, Moon's day, etc. The sun was not worshipped on Sunday, nor the moon on Monday, nor Saturn on Saturday, etc. Also notice carefully that Apollo was not worshipped on Sunday or on any week day. His festival days were *annual*, not weekly, as Adventists have taught. Then note that there was no special reverence for Sunday in pagan times. Here again Adventists are proved to be entirely wrong. This again destroys all their contention that Sunday sacredness originated with pagans. The proof is abundant that no such thing was ever known among the pagan Romans or Greeks. Hence, Sunday-keeping, or Sunday sacredness, could not have originated with them.

Our next witness is from the Smithsonian Institute, Washington, D. C. This great institution of learning is supported by the United States Government. Here the highest qualified specialists in every line of knowledge are employed. Here they have access to every possible means of up-to-date information in the Library of Congress, etc. It will be seen that I addressed nearly the same questions to this learned body and that the answers are the same as from the British Museum:

*Smithsonian Institute, Wash., D. C.,
September 23, 1914.*

REV. D. M. CANRIGHT,
   Grand Rapids, Mich.

   Dear Sir:—I have referred your letter of September 14th to Dr. I. M. Casonawicz, Assistant Curator of Old World Archeology, who furnishes the following replies to your several inquiries:

   Q. 1. Did the pagan Romans and Greeks ever have any regular weekly day of rest from secular work?
   Ans. No.
   2. Did they ever have any weekly festival day?
   Ans. No.
   3. Did they have any regular weekly day when they assembled for pagan worship?

Ans. No.

4. When was our calendar of the week first introduced among the Romans and Greeks?

Ans. The division of the month into weeks was introduced into Rome from Egypt. The date is uncertain, but it was not earlier than the second century, A. D.

5. When was our calendar of the week first recognized in Roman law?

Ans. The earliest Sunday legislation was enacted under Constantine I, 321 A. D. No legislation of earlier date on the division of the month is known.

6. As each day of the week was dedicated to some god, as Sunday to the Sun, Monday to the Moon, Saturday to Saturn, etc., was each of these supposed deities worshipped on one particular day more than any other day?

Ans. No.

7. Did the pagan Romans have any one special day in the week when individuals, if they chose, went to make prayers or offerings to their gods?

Ans. No.

8. Did Apollo have any special day in the week or month more than any other day when he was worshipped with prayers or offerings?

Ans. No.

Very truly yours,
R. RATHBORN,
Assistant Sec. in charge of National Museum.

Here we have two of the most reliable witnesses in the world perfectly agreeing. If their testimony is worth anything, then Adventists must revise their theory that Sunday sacredness, or Sunday festivals, or Sunday rest days originated with pagans.

But here is another witness confirming the other two but giving the answer more in detail. Harvard University, Cambridge, Mass., is the oldest and best known university in America. I addressed the same questions there. George F. Moore, professor of Ancient Roman and Greek History, furnished me the following complete account of all the Roman and Greek festivals. It completely destroys all claim for any pagan sacredness of Sunday.

Professor Moore wrote me as follows:

3 Divinity Ave., Cambridge, Mass.,
May 24, 1913.

Dear Sir:

There are two seven-day weeks: the Jewish week, with a Sabbath on the seventh day; and the Astrological week, with days named after the sun, moon, and five planets, in our order determined by the theories of astrology, but without any day of rest. The combination of the two is Christian. The Astrological week first appears in Greek and Latin writings about the beginning of the Christian era. Its antecedents are unknown. It had no use in ordinary life. Abstinence from labor on the seventh day, or on one day in seven, is a distinctively Jewish institution. The edict of Constantine (321 A. D.) closing the courts on Sunday and prohibiting some kinds of labor on that day, is the first recognition of a seven-day week in Roman law. The ancient Romans had a market day every eight days, when the peasants came to town to market, but it was in *no sense a day of rest*. In the old Roman calendar there were many days when the courts were closed and other public and

private business was not done. They had also many festivals on which the people left their ordinary occupation to take part in the celebrations, but these have *no periodicity like that of the week.*
Very truly yours,
GEORGE F. MOORE.

In a second letter he says:

REV. D. M. CANRIGHT,
Dear Sir:—In reply to your inquiries in your letter of November 23d, I would say:
1. The planetary week in which the days were named from their regents, Saturday, Sunday, etc., was an invention of the *astrologers*, probably in the second century, B. C., and *has no relation to religion or influence upon it.* Saturn, for example, was not worshipped on Saturday, nor Jupiter on Thursday. The festivals of the several gods were *never weekly festivals*, nor did they occur on days fixed by other divisions of the month, say the tenth day.
2. The religious calendars of the Greek cities were independent of one another and underwent many changes in the course of time. Our knowledge of these calendars is incomplete; only that of Athens is pretty fully known. The festivals fell in certain months, and on certain days of the month. Thus, at Athens, where the first month of the year, Hekabombaion, began at the new moon following the summer solstice (roughly corresponding, therefore, to our July), there was a festival of Apollo on the first (or on the seventh of the month). The great festival of Athena Polias, the prophetess of the city, was on the 28th. There were often festivals on the 12th (Kronia) and on the 16th (Synorkia). The second month had only one, rather insignificant,

festival. In the third month, the 5th day was an All Souls' Day, a feast of the dead; a thanksgiving was observed on the 12th-15th; from the 16th to the 25th were the great Athena Elensinia, and so on. No particular days of the month were to be especially favored, either in general or for any individual god.

3. The Roman calendar is preserved only from a comparatively late time, when the worship of Greek and foreign deities was fully established. So far as the *old Roman calendar* can be reconstructed it appears that the Ides of every month were dedicated to Jupiter, who had, besides, festivals on the 23d of April, 5th of July, 19th of August, 11th of October, 25th of December. The festivals of Mars occur chiefly in the month named after him, 1st, 14th, 17th, 19th, 23d, also February 27th, October 15th and 19th. These examples may suffice to show that no principle determines the fixing of these days. It may be observed, however, that, as among many people, the solstices and equinoxes, which mark the seasons of the year, are recognized in the calendar. Also that all who have a calendar based on lunar months give some importance to the first appearance of the new moon, and often to the full moon also.

The festivals were public holidays, each with its own rites, and customs, sacrifices, processions, etc. The priests in Greece and Rome, speaking generally, officiated on these occasions only. The priest was a citizen, elected or chosen by lot, for a longer or shorter time (sometimes for life): in most cases he was not expected to demit his ordinary occupation.

A priesthood who were priests and nothing else, who spent their lives in the service of the temples, with daily offerings and liturgies came in only with foreign, chiefly Oriental, gods, like the *Magna Mater*.

Private persons went to the temples when they had occasion to offer prayers or sacrifices or to make vows, etc. There were no stated days for such visits—though some days were in some temples luckier than others, and there was nothing like a stated day for the assembling of a worshipping congregation except the festivals of the local calendar.

Yours very truly,
GEORGE F. MOORE.

It will readily be seen that this is a valuable historical document covering in detail every phase of Roman and Greek festivals. A weekly Sunday festival was utterly unknown to either pagan nation. No weekly worship or sacredness whatever attached to Sunday. Our Advent brethren, if candid, must abandon that theory.

To make surety doubly sure, I will introduce one more witness. It will be seen that all four fully agree in every item. This one is from Prof. W. H. Westerman, of the University of Wisconsin, Madison, Wis.

University of Wisconsin, Nov. 13, 1913.
REV. D. M. CANRIGHT,
 Grand Rapids, Mich.

Dear Sir:—I shall answer your questions briefly, and in the order in which you sent them.

1. The pagan Greeks and Romans never had a weekly day of rest.
2. They never had a weekly holiday or festival day.
3. They never had a special day in the week on

which they made offerings or prayers to heathen gods. (Neither the pagan Greeks nor the Romans recognized a seven-day division or week division in the month.)

4. They made no offerings or prayers on Sunday to their gods any more than on other days.

5. The seven-day period of dividing the month or the week was never adopted into the calendar of the pagan Greeks. It appears in the Roman calendar after the time of Theodosius, or after 391 A. D., but the week, or seven-day period, first appears in Roman law in a constitution of Constantine, promulgated in 321 A. D. This appears in the Code of Justinian.

The seven-day division of the month, which is, of course from the standpoint of the calendar, a pretty cumbersome method of division, comes from the ancient Hebrews, whose Sabbath, falling on every Saturday, early became a period of rest. The word, Sabbath, means, probably, the "divider." The early Christians, for example, Paul, did not think it necessary for the Christian communities to observe the Jewish Sabbath. Usually, however, they did observe it. In the first two centuries of our era they developed the custom of observing the Lord's Day with prayer and common meals, and out of this, and the Jewish day of rest, arose our practice of observing Sunday.

I have been very glad to be of service to you.

Sincerely yours,

W. H. WESTERMAN.

December 18, 1914.

REV. D. M. CANRIGHT,
  Grand Rapids, Mich.

  Dear Sir:—I will again answer your questions in the order in which you asked them of me.

1. In the constitution of Constantine of A. D. 321, which spoke of the "venerable day of the sun," Constantine regards Sunday as venerable undoubtedly from the Christian standpoint. It had been so regarded by the Christians since the second century, as the day of the Resurrection. It would, therefore, be venerable to Constantine, who had already legalized the Christian religion. If it was in any way venerable or a holiday to the pagans, so far as my information goes, the pagans must have adopted the practice from the Christians.

2. Apollo was not worshipped on any stated day of the week or month more than any other.

3. I do not believe that there is any proof that the early Christians were led to observe Sunday by the example of any pagan worship upon that day. Indeed, I think Tertullian's statements, quoted by you, from Chapter XVI of his "Apology," goes to show that the pagans did not worship the sun upon that day, rather than the opposite.

Very sincerely yours,
W. H. WESTERMAN.

The united testimony of these high authorities is decisive. Neither the pagan Romans nor the Greeks had any weekly day of rest from work, or any weekly festival, or any weekly day for worship. They made no use of a week of seven days for anything. Professor Moore says it had no use in common life. Notice further: The old astrological week of seven days *had no rest day*. The idea of a rest day once a week was unknown to the pagan Romans and Greeks till they learned it of the Jews and Christians centuries after Christ. The edict of Constantine, A. D. 321, was the very first time the week of seven days was recognized in Roman law. All history agrees in this and it is a decisive fact showing that, up to that date, the Romans had made no use of our week of seven days, hence, did not, and could not, have observed Sunday as a day of rest. There was no religious idea connected with the naming of the days from the planets, as Sunday from the sun, Monday from the moon, etc.

All four of these specialists in ancient history agree in answering these questions though neither one knew that they had been submitted to the others; yet all four exactly agree in every particular, though widely scattered, London, Washington, Massachusetts, and Wisconsin. Such an unanimous agreement would settle any question in a court of law.

I accidentally learned that J. W. Moncrieff, A. M., D. D., Associate Professor of Church History, University of Chicago, had carefully studied Seventh-Day Adventism, especially on this subject. So I sent him this chapter for examination. He wrote me as follows:

University of Chicago, May 13, 1915.
Rev. D. M. Canright:
    I appreciate very much the privilege of reading the two chapters of your forthcoming book, and shall certainly want a copy of it when it is out. Seventy years ago, when Seventh-Day Adventism was born, when people possessed a very meager amount of information concerning the ancients, and when even the great Samuel Johnson's Dictionary contained the statement that "The divi-

sion of time by weeks hath been universally observed in the world, not only amongst the civilized, but likewise among the most barbarous, nations" (I quote from the edition of 1819), it was excusable in Seventh-Day Adventists to relate Sunday observance to pagan Roman Sunday observance. But in the last fifty years an enormous amount of research into antiquarian life has been accomplished by reliable, competent historians, and when, with one accord, they proclaim the previously held notion to be a myth, pure and simple, with no support in well ascertained facts, it is high time some one is bringing these facts which are to be found in every recent standard encyclopedia in the articles on "Calendar" and "Week" to the minds of the uninformed who are confused by a doctrine wholly at variance with now ascertained historical fact. I have consulted sixteen encyclopedias and dictionaries, and they differ in no essential detail in their treatment of the subject.

Sincerely yours,
J. W. MONCRIEFF.

It will be seen this historian fully agrees with the four preceding ones. Having given special attention to this particular subject, his testimony is of great value in confirming the other.

I consulted a graduate of Michigan State University who has for four years made a specialty of teaching Roman history in the high school. I asked her if the Romans had any weekly rest day, or day of worship. She said, "No," and gave me "Roman Festivals," by Fowler, as her text book. Two university professors referred me to this same book, so it is good authority. The Preface, page 7, says: "A week of eight days was introduced at an early period." Notice, it was eight days, not seven; and the eighth day was simply a market day, not a day of worship. A large number of festivals are fully described but there is in all the book no reference to any rest day, or day of worship, on Sunday. If there had been such a rest day, the author would certainly have named it.

The Romans, centuries after Christ, learned the week of seven days, partly from Egyptian astrology and partly from Christians and Jews. The "Standard Dictionary," Article "Week," says: "It was not introduced into the Roman calendar till after the reign of Theodosius in the fourth century." The "Universal Dictionary of the English Language," Article "Week," says: "During the early centuries of their history the Greeks and Romans had not the institution of the week."

Webster's Dictionary, Article "Week," says: "The week did not enter into the calendar of the Greeks, and was not introduced at Rome till after the reign of Theodosius." Constantine had been dead over forty years before Theodosius began to reign. So at the time when Constantine issued his Sunday law, A. D. 321, his pagan subjects did not use the week of seven days, hence, could not have kept the first day of our week till taught it by Christians and required by Constantine's law.

Prof. A. Rauschenbusch, of Rochester Theological Seminary, quotes Lotz thus: "It is a vain thing to attempt to prove that the Greeks and Romans had anything resembling the Sabbath. Such opinion is refuted even by this, that the Roman writers ridicule the Sabbath as something peculiar to the Jews. In proof he cites many passages from the Roman poets, and one from Tacitus. Seneca also condemned the Sabbath observance of the Jews as a waste of time by which a seventh part of life was lost."[1] Herzog says: "No special religious celebration of any one day of the week can be pointed out in any one of the pagan religions" (Article "Sabbath").

The renowned Max Muller in "Chips from a German Work Shop," Vol. V, page 116, says: "It is well known that the names of the seven days of the week are derived from the names of the planets, and it is equally well known that in Europe the system of weeks and week days is comparatively of very modern origin. It was not a Greek, nor a Roman, nor a Hindu, but a Jewish or Babylonian invention."

The early Christian Father, Tertullian, A. D. 200, bears a decisive testimony that the pagans had no weekly festival, did not keep the Lord's Day with Christians. Reproving Christians for attending heathen feasts, he says: "Oh, truer fealty of the heathen to their own religion which taketh to itself no rite of the Christians. We are not afraid lest we be openly declared to be heathen! If thou must needs have some indulgence for the flesh too, thou hast it and thou hast not only as many days as

[1] "Saturday or Sunday," p. 83.

they, but even more. For the heathen festival is on *but one day in every year, thine upon every eighth day.* Gather out the several solemn feasts of the heathen and set them out in order; they will not be able to make up a pentecost."[1]

Notice that he says the heathen did not have a festival on the Lord's Day, nor on Pentecost, and that the heathen festivals came only "*once a year*," not every week, like the Christian Day. He says that all their feast days, if gathered together, would not be as much as Pentecost. This is decisive, that the heathen did not have a weekly festival day, nor did they have a festival on the same day the Christians did; viz., on the Lord's Day.

Johnson's "New Universal Encyclopedia," Article "Week," says: "The Greeks divided the month into periods of ten days, and the Romans gathered the days into periods of eight days; with both, the first day of a period was market day, on which country people came to town and stirred up both business and public life. The period of seven days, the week proper, was introduced to the Romans and Greeks, partly by Christianity, partly by Egyptian astronomy."

This demolishes the theory that keeping the first day of our Christian week came to Christians from the pagan Romans. Exactly the opposite is true. The Jew and Christians taught it to the pagan Romans.

Schaff, in his "Church History," says: "The

[1] "Ante-Niciune Lib.," Vol. XI, pp. 162-163.

pagan Romans paid no more regard to the Christian Sunday than to the Jewish Sabbath."

The "Encyclopedia Americana," Article "Week," says: "The Romans and Greeks each divided the months into periods, and were not acquainted with the week till a late period. The Romans had, however, for civil uses, as the arrangement of market days, a cycle of eight days, the ninth being the recurring one, instead of the eighth as with us."

I have before me a book of 160 pages, entitled, "Sunday is the Christian Sabbath, or Lord's Day," by M. H. MacLead, Pueblo, Colo. It is the most exhaustive and scholarly work I have yet found on the history of the Sunday question in the first four centuries. He carefully quotes a large number of high authorities showing that the pagan Romans and Greeks had no weekly day of rest or worship on any day of the week. On the subject of heathen rest days he says: "I have given it an uncompromising consideration. It was not without a study of the matter that I ventured even to myself a final and unchangeable denial of any truth in the claim." What the ancient Egyptians, Babylonians, or other ancient nations believed or did has nothing to do with our question. It is claimed by Adventists that Sunday, as a day of rest and worship, came into the Church from pagan Rome. Hence, that is the only question to settle. The simple fact that Sunday was named from the sun, dedicated to the sun, or was sacred to the sun, does not furnish the slightest evidence that people ceased work on that day. Every day in the work was named from some supposed deity and was sacred to that god. "The World's Standard Dictionary" says: "Monday, the day sacred to the moon." Did pagans worship the moon that day? Did they cease work that day? Saturday was Saturn's day, sacred to Saturn. Did they rest that day? So of all the days of the week. If they rested every day named after some god, when would they work? Sunday was no more sacred than any other day and pagans reverenced none.

So plain is the evidence on this subject that some of the best read Adventists have admitted that pagans did not rest from work on Sunday. Thus Elder J. H. Waggoner says of Constantine's Sunday law, A. D. 321: "Though the venerable day of the sun had long—very long—been venerated by them and their heathen ancestors, the idea of rest from worldly labor in his worship was entirely new."[1] Mark this confession, for it gives up the main pillar of their argument in their effort to prove that Sunday-keeping was taken from the pagans. The pagans never kept Sunday. It was a *new idea* to them when they were required to cease work that day! Where did they get that new idea? From the emperor who had just recently professed Christianity. He got it from his Christian brethren who had always kept it! See the folly of arguing that the pagans taught Christians to keep Sunday, when the pagans them-

[1] "Replies to Elder Canright," p. 130.

selves had never kept it. Here is another confession:

Elder L. R. Conradi, Seventh-Day Adventist, author of "History of the Sabbath," edition of 1912, in a letter to me dated Hamburg, February 9, 1914, says: "A weekly rest day from work and solely dedicated to divine worship was unknown in heathenism and only known among the people of Israel." In answer to my question, "Did the pagan Romans keep Sunday as a religious day?" he says: "We never claimed that. The idea of keeping a day means, in the present age, resting from work and giving the time solely to worship. *But this the pagans never did.* They only made prayers to the sun-god and then followed their regular work."

Here we have two witnesses from Seventh-Day Adventists themselves, confessing that the pagans had no weekly day of rest from common work. Of course, they could say nothing else, for all history says the same. So then this point is settled beyond denial.

"Admissions in favor of truth from the ranks of its enemies constitute the highest kind of evidence." These confessions from the two Adventist elders give up the question, as any candid person must see.

Elder Conradi, above quoted, says of the pagans: "They only made prayers to the sun-god and then followed their regular work." Here he assumes that the pagans made Sunday a special day of worship when they made prayers to the sun-god. He asserts that for which there is not a particle of proof. No prayers were made to the heathen gods on Sunday more than on Saturday or any other day. He cannot produce a scrap of proof for his assertion. The quotations given above from the historians of the several universities squarely deny what he asserts without any proof. Did all these pagans leave their homes every Sunday and go to their temples and offer prayers? No. They had no meetings whatever that day, nor on any other day of the week. On some special occasion, as a birthday, or recovery from sickness, or to avert some feared evil, or on some yearly festival, persons would go and offer incense or gifts to the gods. That was all. There was no regular day in the week for any offerings of gifts or prayers. The Adventists have invented a pagan Sunday of rest and worship which never existed.

No pagan nation to-day keeps Sunday. The great Chinese nation, numbering four hundred millions, keeps no day. Elder W. A. Westworth, Seventh-Day Adventist, in the Battle Creek, Mich., *Daily Journal*, May 18, 1914, says: "I have put in 15,000 miles in inland China visiting our stations. The Chinese have no week, nor any day of the week, kept as a weekly rest." The same is true of the Japanese, 67,000,000, the Koreans, the millions of pagans in Africa, etc. Then the Mohammedans, numbering 200,000,000, rest on Friday, and all work on Saturday and Sunday. They copied the idea of a weekly rest day from the Jews

PAGANS HAD NO SUNDAY WORSHIP 125

and Christians in the seventh century after Christ. India has a population of 315,000,000. They have no weekly rest day. The entire population of the earth is sixteen hundred millions. Of these only six hundred millions believe in the Bible and Christianity, and hence nominally respect Sunday. So ten hundred millions, nearly two-thirds of the people on the globe, have no regard for Sunday or Saturday and never had. All on this globe who now, or at any other time, have ever rested on Sunday have learned it from Christians. So Christians could never have learned it from pagans, for none of them ever kept Sunday.

The observers of the seventh day continually assert that Sunday with pagans was always a popular festival day, a day for religious assemblies and pagan worship, then of festivity or, perhaps, work, by some. The above testimony from numerous reliable authors squarely contradicts these assertions. Listen now to the Adventists. Of Sunday they say: "They are assembly days at early morn, then given up to busy pleasure and to labor." "Many of his [Constantine's] pagan subjects reverenced the same day as a day of prayer in honor of the sun." Again: "The very effect of joining the pagans in their devotions on Sunday was to let down the bars which God had put up."[1] Here is another: "The bishops would very readily adopt the most popular heathen festival day [Sun-

---

[1] "History of the Sabbath," edition 1912, pp. 373, 384, 385, 363.

day] in order to gain the favor of the pagans." "The observance of Sunday was itself the custom which was brought into the Church by converts from heathenism." "Sunday the wild solar holiday of all pagan times."[1]

Here is one from a Seventh-Day Baptist, Rev. A. H. Lewis, in "History of the Sabbath and Sunday," page 70: "Sunday, already a festival among the heathen." "The sun's day had been a leading weekly pagan festival for many centuries" (page 521). Elder Andrews in "Testimony of the Fathers," pages 26, 34, 43, says: "The Roman people observed a festival on the first day of the week." "The day commonly honored as a festival by the Romans."

These are only samples of what is repeated over and over by opposers of the Lord's Day. These assertions are made, not only without proof, but directly contrary to all reliable testimony, as we have quoted above. There was absolutely nothing of the kind with Romans or Greeks.

Elder Waggoner says: "Sunday is in *every feature* a heathen institution."[2] Let us see. What are the features of Sunday as kept by Christians? 1. All secular work ceases. 2. People dress up and go to church. 3. A hymn is sung. 4. Prayer is offered. 5. Scriptures are read. 6. A sermon is preached. 7. A collection

---

[1] "Fathers of the Catholic Church," by E. J. Waggoner, pp. 324, 326, 328.

[2] "Replies to Canright," p. 133.

PAGANS HAD NO SUNDAY WORSHIP 127

is taken. 8. The Lord's Supper is celebrated. 9. Benediction is pronounced. These are the *features* of the Christian observance of Sunday. Waggoner says that in *every feature* it is pagan! How many of these features can be found in the pagan day? Absolutely not one. They did not even cease work that day as he himself says above. Is not his assertion recklessly untrue? Could the pagan Romans give to the Christians these features of Sunday observance when they themselves never had one of them? It is absurd. But Adventists believe and teach it as a fact while all reliable evidence shows that it is all absolutely untrue.

The strong, clear, united historical quotations given in this chapter prove, beyond denial, that the pagan Romans never had any religious regard for Sunday, never had the week of seven days in common life, or in their calendar, or in their civil or religious laws. The very first deference they ever paid to Sunday was in obedience to the law of Constantine the first Christian emperor.

Because one day was named Sunday, sun's day, and because the ancient Babylonians and others worshipped the sun, therefore Adventists always assume and assert that Sunday was specially devoted to the worship of the sun. Thus one writer says: "The worship of the sun is one of the oldest and most universal forms of idolatry, and Sunday was the special day honored by the sun worshipper." Another writer says: "The very name Sunday is a standing witness that it was the day of sun worship." This is simply in the sound of names, nothing more, without any foundation, in fact.

This ready assumption is entirely groundless. Each day of the week was named from some planet: as Sunday from the sun, Monday from the moon, Saturday from Saturn, etc. The first hour of each day was supposed to be ruled over by the planet of that day. This was purely an astrological invention for civil purposes and had no religious significance whatever; no idea of worship was connected with the name of any one of these days. Religious worship had nothing to do in naming the days. The idea was purely and only astrological. Thus Johnson's "New Universal Encyclopedia," Article "Week," says: "It was found as a civil institution in the very earliest times among the Hindoos, Persians, Assyrians, and Egyptians. But the Jews were the only nation with which the week had a religious significance." So also the answers from the above quoted historians all agree that names of the days are purely astrological, not religious. Sun worship had no connection with Sunday whatever, no more than any other day.

VI

HISTORICAL EVIDENCE THAT OUR LORD'S DAY WAS OBSERVED FROM THE TIME OF THE APOSTLES

WE will now present historical evidence, proving that the observance of the first day of the week, as a day of worship, was universal among Christians in the days immediately following the apostles. If Sunday observance existed here, then it did not originate several hundred years later with Constantine, or with the Papacy. We will begin soon after the close of the New Testament.

PLINY'S LETTER, A. D. 107

Pliny was governor of Bithynia, Asia Minor, A. D. 106–108. He wrote A. D. 107 to Trajan, the emperor, concerning the Christians, thus: "They were wont to meet together, on a *stated day* before it was light, and sing among themselves alternately a hymn to Christ as God. . . . When these things were performed, it was their custom to separate and then to come together again to a meal which they ate in common without any disorder."[1] That this was Sunday is evident. 1. They came together to worship Christ. 2. They assembled to

[1] Horne's "Introduction," Vol. I, Chap. iii, Sec. 2, p. 84.

eat a meal together, the Lord's Supper. The "stated day" for this was Sunday. "Upon the first day of the week when the disciples came together to break bread" (Acts xx. 7). This is exactly parallel to Pliny's statement.

Eusebius, the historian, A. D. 324, says: "I think that he [the Psalmist] describes the morning assemblies in which we are accustomed to assemble throughout the world." "By this is prophetically signified the service which is performed very early and every morning of the resurrection day throughout the whole world."[1] This is exactly what Pliny says: They met together "on a stated day before it was light;" they assembled to eat together a meal. Eusebius says it was the custom of all Christians "to meet very early and every morning of the resurrection day." This ought to settle it and does. Pliny's stated day was Sunday. This was in the very region where the apostles labored, and only *eleven* years after St. John died.

The "Advent History of the Sabbath," edition of 1912, is compelled to admit that Sunday observance was in the Christian Church at the beginning of the second century. The author says: "The results of our investigation concerning the origin of Sunday [is] that it was not introduced into the Christian Church until the beginning of the second century" (page 450). That is exactly the date when Pliny wrote,—immediately following the death of the last apostle.

[1] "Sabbath Manual," p. 125.

BARNABAS, A. D. 120

This epistle was highly prized in the earliest Churches, read in some of them as part of Scripture, and is found in the oldest manuscript of the Scriptures, *namely the Sinaitic*. That it was written by a pious man of learning and influence cannot be doubted.

Johnson's "New Universal Encyclopedia" says: "It is frequently cited by the Fathers, and was by many regarded as being of authority in the Church; some even claiming for it a place in the sacred canon."

This is a summary of the best modern criticism as to the date, character and authority of the epistle of Barnabas. Read and reverenced in the Church as next to the Gospels themselves as early as A. D. 120, or within twenty-four years of the death of St. John, it shows what Christians believed and practiced immediately after the apostles. In this epistle we read: "Incense is a vain abomination unto me, and your new moons and Sabbaths I cannot endure. He has, therefore, abolished these things" (Chapter II). Elder Andrews admits that "he presently asserts the abolition of the Sabbath of the Lord."[1] Coming to the first day of the week, Barnabas says: "Wherefore, also, we keep the eighth day with joyfulness, the day, also, on which Jesus rose again from the dead" (Chapter XV).

Notice this fact: All admit that this epistle of

[1] "Testimony," etc., p. 22.

Barnabas was in existence in the beginning of the second century, or not later than the middle of it. At that time it was supposed by the Churches to have been written as a part of the New Testament Scriptures. It is in the oldest copy of the Bible right after Revelation. It states in positive terms that the Jewish Sabbath was abolished and that Christians kept the day of the resurrection. Now would the Churches, week after week, read this language as inspired, and then not keep Sunday? That is not reasonable. Hence this book does show what Christians believed and practiced at that date, A. D. 120.

But Adventists say this writing was a forgery. It was no such thing. There is not a word in the whole epistle claiming that the author was the apostle Barnabas. No name is attached to it nor is there any claim that it was written by an apostle. For some reason, not now known, it came to be attributed to Barnabas. The book of Hebrews has no name to it; it is supposed that Paul wrote it and we accept it as such, but some doubt it, and it cannot be proved. Shall we call it a forgery? Just as well as to call the epistle of Barnabas a forgery.

Here, once for all, we will notice the chief argument on which Adventists depend to invalidate the testimony of all the early Fathers in favor of the Lord's Day. They try to show that Barnabas, Justin Martyr, Origen, etc., held some notions which none of us now believe. Hence their testimony must be unreliable. This argument they repeat over and over at great length in the case of every early writer who witnesses for Sunday. Now it occurs that one of their writers, Elder J. H. Waggoner, when it happens to suit his purpose, has himself answered this argument. Of the Reformers he says: "We think the Reformers retained a grievous error of their early training; but that does not invalidate their testimony in regard to a *matter of fact* with which they were well acquainted." [1]

Now apply that to the early Fathers. They lived there, and state over and over, all agreeing in it, that they themselves and all Christians then observed Sunday. This was a simple matter of *fact* with which they were well acquainted. Waggoner says such testimony is reliable. Of course it is. It proves beyond question that the Lord's Day was an unquestioned practice of the early Church.

We do not quote these Fathers to prove a doctrine; for that we go only to the Bible. We quote them to prove a simple, historical fact, viz.: that the early Christians did keep Sunday, hence it could not have started with the Popes centuries later.

THE TEACHING OF THE APOSTLES, A. D. 125

This was not written by the apostles; yet its date is very early. Some place it as early as A. D. 80.

[1] "Replies to Canright," p. 164.

Professor Harnack, of Berlin, says many place it between A. D. 90, and A. D. 120. This is the date most favored. It cannot be much later. The New York *Independent* says of it: "By all odds the most important writing exterior to New Testament." Prof. D. R. Dungan, President of Drake University, says: "It is evident that it is not far on this side of the death of the apostle John." The noted scholar, Rev. Wilbur F. Crafts, in his "Sabbath for Man," page 383, says: It was "written, as the best scholars almost unanimously agree, not later than forty years after the death of the last of the apostles, and during the lifetime of many who had heard John's teaching." In the preface to this important document, the editors, Professors Hitchcock and Brown in the Union Theological Seminary, New York, say: "The genuineness of the document can hardly be doubted." "The document belongs undoubtedly to the second century; possibly as far back as 120 A. D.; hardly later than 160" (Introduction).

Chapter fourteen of the "Teaching of the Apostles" says: "But every Lord's Day do ye gather yourselves together, and break bread, and give thanksgiving," etc. This testimony is clear and decisive that the Lord's Day was the established day of worship, at that early day.

JUSTIN MARTYR, A. D. 140

I quote from "The Testimony of the Fathers," by Elder Andrews: "Justin's 'Apology' was

JUSTIN MARTYR　　135

written at Rome about the year 140," "and this at a distance of only forty-four years from the date of John's vision upon Patmos." "It does not appear that Justin, and those at Rome who held with him in doctrine, paid the slightest regard to the ancient Sabbath. He speaks of it as abolished, and treats it with contempt" (page 33).

This is the confession which even the historian of the Seventh-Day Adventists is compelled to make. The Jewish Sabbath was disregarded by Christians within forty-four years of the death of the last apostle. And this is proven by the testimony of an eminent Christian minister who lived right there.

Justin in his "Apology" for them to the emperor fairly represented what Christians generally held then, just as he should have done. Elder Andrews conveys the impression that Justin represented only a small party of apostate Christians at Rome and that he is quite unreliable. But the facts are just the reverse. He was a Greek, born in Palestine and held his "Dialogue with Trypho" at Ephesus, Asia Minor, in the church where St. John lived and died, the very center of the Eastern Church, and only forty-four years after John's death. Of Justin the "Encyclopedia Americana" says: "One of the earliest and most learned writers of the Christian Church. . . . He was also equally zealous in opposing alleged heretics." "Schaff-Herzog Encyclopedia" says: "In these works Justin professes to present the system of doctrine held by *all*

Christians and seeks to be orthodox on all points. The only difference he knows of as existing between Christians concerned the millennium. Thus Justin is an incontrovertible witness for the unity of the faith in the Church of his day, and to the fact that the Gentile type of Christianity prevailed."

Notice carefully: At that date, A. D. 140, the only difference among Christians was about the millennium. Then they must all have agreed in keeping Sunday, as Justin says that was the day all kept as we will soon see.

"Eusebius says that he overshadowed all the great men who illuminated the second century by the splendor of his name." His writings are "the most important that have come to us from the second century."[1]

Doctor Schaff says of him: "After his conversion Justin devoted himself wholly to the vindication of the Christian religion, as an *itinerant* evangelist, with no fixed abode."[2] Not only were his books accepted without dispute as expressing the practice of the Church, but his itinerant life, now in Palestine, then in Rome, Greece and Ephesus, enabled him to know this practice, and stamps his testimony with a force equal to demonstration. So, then, Justin is an unimpeachable witness for the faith and practice of Christians

---

[1] McClintock and Strong's "Encyclopedia," Article "Justin Martyr."
[2] "Church History," Vol. I, p. 482.

generally a few years after the death of the apostles.

Now hear what Justin says about the first day of the week: "And on the day called Sunday, all who live in cities or in the country gather together to one place, and the memoirs of the apostles or the writings of the prophets are read, as long as time permits; then, when the reader has ceased, the president verbally instructs and exhorts to the imitation of these good things. Then we all rise together and pray, and, as we before said, when our prayer is ended, bread and wine and water are brought, and the president in like manner offers prayers and thanksgivings, according to his ability, and the people assent, saying, Amen; and there is a distribution to each, and a participation of that over which thanks have been given, and to those who are absent a portion is sent by the deacons. And they who are well to do, and willing, give what each thinks fit; and what is collected is deposited with the president, who succors the orphans and widows, and those who, through sickness or any other cause, are in want, and those who are in bonds, and the strangers sojourning among us, and, in a word, takes care of all who are in need. But Sunday is the day on which we all hold our common assembly, because it is the first day on which God, having wrought a change in the darkness and matter, made the world; and Jesus Christ, our Saviour, on the same day rose from the dead. For He was crucified on the day before that of Saturn (Saturday); and on the day after that of Saturn, which is the day of the sun, having appeared to His apostles and disciples, He taught them these things, which we have submitted to you also for your consideration."[1]

This "Apology" was written by Justin when Christians were being terribly persecuted. It was addressed to Antoninus, the emperor, "also to the sacred senate and the *whole Roman people* in behalf of those who of *all nations* are now unjustly hated and aspersed."[2]

It was in behalf of the entire Christian Church in all the vast Roman Empire, as he plainly states. Hence it presents the practice of the general Church, not simply a local church at Rome as Adventists unfairly state. It was addressed to the Roman emperor and the senate to correctly inform them of the faith and practice of Roman Christian subjects. Justin was martyred because he would not sacrifice to pagan gods. Notice that he says that, "On the day called Sunday, *all who live in the cities*, or *in the country* gather together to one place," etc. "But Sunday is the day on which *we all* hold our common assembly." This practice was general among all Christians as far as he had travelled, and he was an itinerant preacher like Moody, or General Booth of the Salvation Army. Hence this is positive proof that Sunday-keeping was general in the Christian Church at that early

[1] "The First Apology of Justin," Chap. xlvii.
[2] Eusebius, "Eccl. History," Book IV, Chap. xii, p. 139.

date. Justin does not state simply his opinion, but a *fact* then existing, viz., that all Christians " whether in cities or country " " in all nations " held their assemblies on Sunday.

Justin does not call Sunday the Sabbath nor the Lord's Day! This is readily answered by the fact that Justin was writing to a heathen emperor who would have been wholly ignorant of the meaning of either of those terms. But there the naked facts stand, clear, positive and undeniable, that within forty-four years after the book of Revelation was written Christians did hold their assemblies on Sunday. And Justin says that Jesus taught these things to the apostles.

Probably the Jewish Christians did continue to observe the Sabbath the same as they did other Jewish customs for a time. But even these also kept the Lord's Day as will be seen later.

Justin plainly states that the Gentile believers did not keep the Sabbath. He says: " The Gentiles who have believed on Him, although they neither keep the Sabbath, nor are circumcised, nor observe the feasts " yet are God's children.'

So to-day: go to any part of the globe and wherever you find Christians of any sect or nation, there you find them keeping Sunday. A few Sabbatarians of late origin are the only exceptions to this. How did this universal custom come about if not started at the very foundation of the Church by the apostles themselves?

[1] " Dialogue with Trypho," Chap. xxvi.

DIONYSIUS, BISHOP OF CORINTH IN GREECE, A. D. 170

But we will hear further from these Fathers themselves as to whether they kept Sunday. Dionysius, Bishop of Corinth, the Church which Paul raised up and to which he gave the command about Sunday collections, 1 Cor. xvi. 1–2, says: "We passed this holy Lord's Day, in which we read your letter, from the constant reading of which we shall be able to draw admonition."[1] That the Lord's Day is the resurrection day we have seen. This term is never applied to any other than the first day. Notice that this witness is from Greece, not Rome. So the resurrection day was a "holy" day, A. D. 170.

In this chapter Eusebius gives quite a lengthy account of Dionysius as a most devoted Christian, a bishop of great and wide influence. He warned others against all heresies in many letters he wrote. Eusebius quotes his exact words about the "Holy Lord's Day" as above. As these letters were sent to many other Churches it shows that the Lord's Day was by all regarded as a holy day.

BARDESANES OF EDESSA, SYRIA, A. D. 180

Coming down only ten years later, we have the testimony of the heretic Bardesanes, the Syrian, who flourished about A. D. 180. He belonged to the sect of the Gnostics which was very numerous all over the far East. He says: "What then shall we say respecting the new race of ourselves who

[1] Eusebius, "Eccl. History," Book IV, Chap. xxiii.

are Christians, whom in every country, and in every region the Messiah established at His coming? For, lo, wherever we be, all of us are called by the one name of the Messiah, Christians, and upon one day, which is the first day of the week, we assemble ourselves together."[1]

Notice that these Christians were scattered widely "in every country and every region." Bardesanes says just the same as Justin Martyr, "We assemble ourselves together" upon the first day of the week. These two witnesses are much alike as to Sunday. Justin, strictly orthodox, says that "all in cities and country" assemble on Sunday. Bardesanes, heretic, says the same for all the countries of the far East. The observance of Sunday was general both among orthodox and heretics.

Notice here also a refutation of the idea so strongly urged by Sabbatarians, that Sunday-keeping originated at Rome, and was for a long time confined there. Elder Andrews has to admit that the Gnostics at this date used Sunday as a day of worship. But, 1. The Gnostics were emphatically an *eastern* sect, originating in Syria, and were most numerous in Alexandria, Asia Minor, and the East. Rome never had any influence over them. Bardesanes himself lived at Edessa, in Mesopotamia, 2,500 miles east of Rome, on another continent, under another nation. 2. This sect was numerous in the East as early as A. D. 150, or fifty-five years after the death of John. So we have Sunday-keep-

[1] "Laws of Countries," A. D. 180.

ing not only at Rome, but all over the East as early as A. D. 150, hundreds of years before there was any "Pope" at Rome.

No exception to this can be found whether orthodox or heretic. All observe the Lord's Day. Even Sabbatarians are compelled to admit this. Elder Andrews says: "Those Fathers who hallow the Sabbath do generally associate with it the festival called by them the Lord's Day."[1]

Yes, while some did, for a while, keep the Sabbath, yet even they, in every instance, also kept the Lord's Day.

CLEMENT OF ALEXANDRIA, EGYPT, A. D. 194

Clement was one of the most celebrated of the Christian Fathers. He writes about A. D. 194. He says: "He, in fulfillment of the precept, keeps the Lord's Day when he abandons an evil disposition, and assumes that of the Gnostic, glorifying the Lord's resurrection in himself" (Book VII, Chapter XII). The Lord's Day, it will be seen here, and all along, is the resurrection day. Clement lived, not at Rome, but in Egypt. So Sunday-keeping was not simply a Roman usage, as Adventists claim.

Adventists seek to discredit Clement's testimony about the Lord's Day by saying that he was influenced by Greek philosophy as taught by Plato, Socrates, etc. But this is easily answered by the fact that neither the Greeks in general, nor any of the philosophers, ever practiced, or taught, any ob-

[1] "Testimony of the Fathers," p. 11.

servance of Sunday. They never knew anything about a weekly day of rest or worship. The weekly calendar was unknown to them till taught it by Christians at a later date. (See Chapter V.) Hence, whatever else Clement and the Church at Alexandria gathered from Greek philosophers, they did not get the Lord's Day from them. When they adopted Christianity they accepted the Lord's Day as a part of it. Heathen Gnosticism knew nothing of any weekly rest day; hence, Christian Gnostics could not get their Lord's Day from them.

TERTULLIAN OF AFRICA, A. D. 200

Tertullian was one of the most noted of the early Fathers. Was born A. D. 160. He was highly educated, bred to the law, and very talented. Brought up a pagan, he was converted to Christ and vehemently opposed heathenism ever after. Radically severe in his principles, opposed to all conformity to the world, the laxity of the Roman Church drove him to withdraw from it, which he ever after hotly opposed. So he was not a Romanist, nor did Rome have a particle of influence over him only to drive him the other way. He was strictly orthodox in faith and a lover of the Scriptures. Hence if it were true that Sunday-keeping, as a heathen institution, was being introduced into the Church by Rome, Tertullian is just the man who would have opposed and fearlessly condemned it.

Johnson's "Cyclopedia" says of him: "One of the greatest men of the early Church." He "joined the Puritanic sect of the Montanists. They were orthodox in doctrine, but stern in spirit and discipline." "He remained true to the faith of the Catholics, but fought them vehemently on matters of morality and discipline. He was also a representative of the African opposition to Rome." The "Schaff-Herzog Cyclopedia" says of him: "One of the grandest and most original characters of the ancient Church." "*Greek philosophy he despised.*" Of his great book they say: "One of the magnificent monuments of the ancient Church." Authon's "Classical Dictionary" says of him: "He informs us more correctly than any other writer respecting the Christian doctrines of his time. . . . Tertullian was held in very high esteem by the subsequent Fathers of the Church." Neander says: "Tertullian is a writer of peculiar importance."[1]

Here then is a competent and unimpeachable witness to the doctrines and practices of the universal Church, A. D. 200, or only 104 years after John.

Tertullian says: "We solemnize the day after Saturday in contradistinction to those who call this day their Sabbath, and devote it to ease and eating, deviating from the old Jewish customs, which they are now very ignorant of."[2] Tertullian again declares that his brethren did not observe the days held sacred by the Jews: "We neither accord with the Jews in their peculiarities in regard to food, nor

---

[1] Rose's "Neander," p. 424.
[2] Tertullian's "Apology," Chap. xvi.

in their sacred days." "We, however (just as we have received), only on the day of the Lord's resurrection ought to guard not only against kneeling, but every posture and office of solicitude; deferring even our business, lest we give any place to the devil."[1] Sunday, then, was observed by Christians at that early date, but Saturday was not.

The above testimony of this great Christian teacher is clear, positive, and decisive. The Jewish Sabbath was not kept; the Lord's Day was. Tertullian was one of the greatest Christian teachers of that day, A. D. 200. Could it be that these influential leaders taught and practiced thus, while all the Churches believed and did just the other way? That is, kept the Jewish Sabbath and did not keep the Lord's Day? Might as well say that Moody and Spurgeon taught Sunday observance while none of their followers believed it.

In the case of Tertullian, the last edition of the "Advent History of the Sabbath" devotes twelve large pages trying to discredit him. Why? Because his testimony is squarely against them and they fear it. It is a significant fact that Adventists do not find even one single Christian writer or leader for hundreds of years after Christ who is worthy of any reliance! All are fools, forgers, unreliable, apostates, semi-pagans, etc.! Why this effort to impeach them all? The reason is easy to find—all bear a decided witness against Sabbatarian teachings.

[1] "Tertullian on Prayer," Chap. xxiii.

ORIGEN, A. D. 225

Origen (about A. D. 225) was a man of immense learning, and his writings are numerous. "Origen may well be pronounced one of the ablest and worthiest of the church Fathers."[1]

The following items about Origen are gathered from the "Schaff-Herzog Encyclopedia." He was born at Alexandria, A. D. 185. Was carefully trained by Christian parents. His father was martyred. He was one of the most learned men of his age. He was devoutly pious. He became the teacher of the greatest men of his time, even teaching bishops and emperors. He travelled extensively to Rome, Arabia, Antioch, Greece, Tyre, Cappadocia; Jerusalem, Cæsarea, etc. Hence he was familiar with all the customs of Christians everywhere. This makes his testimony to the Lord's Day at that early date reliable and of great importance. He says: "If it be objected to us on this subject that we ourselves are accustomed to observe certain days, as, for example, the Lord's Day, the preparation, the passover, or pentecost."[2]

In his commentary on Exodus, Par. 5, he says: "It is plain from Holy Writ that manna was first given on earth on the Lord's Day. But if it be clear from the Holy Scriptures that God rained manna from Heaven on the Lord's Day, and rained none on the Sabbath Day, let the Jews understand that from that time our Lord's Day was set above

---

[1] McClintock and Strong's "Encyclopedia."
[2] "Origen against Celsus," Book VIII, Chap. xxii.

the true Sabbath—for on our Lord's Day God always rains down manna from Heaven; for the discourses which are delivered to us are from Heaven."

Here Origen shows that the Jewish Sabbath was set aside, and the Lord's Day was the superior day, the day on which Christians assembled to hear discourses from God's ministers. This agrees with Justin Martyr, Tertullian, and all as above. Notice that this witness is from the East, not from pagan Rome. Origen was a Greek, not a Latin. As Origen travelled extensively among the Churches and preached for them, and his books were read by them, it shows that the observance of the Lord's Day was general among them all. He would not have been everywhere invited to preach for them if they had not believed as he did.

THE APOSTOLICAL CONSTITUTIONS, A. D. 250

Of the "Apostolical Constitutions" (A. D. 250) Elder Andrews, Adventist, says: "The so-called 'Apostolical Constitutions' were not the work of the apostles, but they were in existence as early as the third century, and were then very generally believed to express the doctrine of the apostles. They do therefore furnish important historical testimony to the practice of the Church at that time. Mosheim, in his 'Historical Commentaries,' Cent. 1, section 51, speaks thus of these 'constitutions': 'The matter of this work is unquestionably ancient; since the manners and discipline of which it exhibits a view are those which prevailed among the Christians of the second and third centuries, especially those resident in Greece and the oriental regions.'"[1] Notice again that this work was the product of the Eastern Church and hence shows the custom of the Church in the East instead of that at Rome.

These, then, will be good witnesses to the practice of the Church about A. D. 250. In section 7, paragraph 59, we read: "And on the day of our Lord's resurrection, which is the Lord's Day, meet more diligently, sending praise to God that made the universe by Jesus and sent Him to us." "Otherwise what apology will He make to God who does not assemble on that day to hear the saving word concerning the resurrection." In Book VII, section 2, paragraph 30, he says: "On the day of the resurrection of the Lord, that is, the Lord's Day, assemble yourselves together, without fail, giving thanks to God," etc. In the same paragraph, in speaking of the resurrection of Christ, the writer says: "On which account we solemnly assemble to celebrate the feast of the resurrection on the Lord's Day," etc.

These testimonies are decisive, and do show beyond a doubt that the Christians of those early days used the Lord's Day just as it is used now for religious worship.

CYPRIAN, BISHOP OF CARTHAGE, A. D. 253

Cyprian was one of the greatest scholars and men of influence in all Christendom about seventy-

[1] "Testimony," etc., p. 13.

five years before the date of Constantine's edict of A. D. 321. He was a most devoted Christian, had great wealth, half of which he gave to the poor. Refusing to reverence the pagan idols, he was martyred. He opposed the Roman Church and bishop. Of him the "Schaff-Herzog Encyclopedia" says: "At the time when the controversy concerning baptism broke out between him and Bishop Stephen of Rome (255) Cyprian stood undoubtedly as the prominent and most influential leader in the Christian Church." "The Papacy was not yet born."

Of this great leader, the "Advent History of the Sabbath" (1912) says: "The next Father offering an argument for Sunday is Cyprian" (page 370). Hence there is no doubt that Cyprian kept the Lord's Day and defended it. He said: "Because the eighth day, that is, the first day after the Sabbath, was to be that on which the Lord should rise again, and should quicken us, and give us circumcision of the Spirit; the eighth day, that is, the first day after the Sabbath, and the Lord's Day, which went before in the figure."[1]

Did not the Churches practice as this great leader did and taught? Surely. Then they kept the Lord's Day sixty years before Constantine's conversion, a generation before his Sunday law. Notice that Cyprian lived in Africa, not at Rome, and that he opposed Rome.

[1] Cyprian's "Epistles," No. 58, Sect. 4.

ANATOLIUS, A. D. 270, BISHOP OF LAODICEA, ASIA

He was Bishop of Laodicea, Asia Minor. Not a Roman, but a Greek. This Church was raised up by Paul himself, and must have been well acquainted with the apostle's doctrine. In his seventh canon Anatolius says: "The obligation of the Lord's resurrection binds us to keep the paschal festival on the Lord's Day." In his tenth canon he uses this language: "The solemn festival of the resurrection of the Lord can be celebrated only on the Lord's Day." In his sixteenth canon he says: "Our regard for the Lord's resurrection which took place on the Lord's Day will lead us to celebrate it on the same principle." See how all these early Christians call the resurrection day "the Lord's Day" and how they honor it. How entirely different from our Sabbatarians who can hardly find terms mean enough by which to express their contempt for Sunday! Why is this difference and what does it show?

VICTORINUS, BISHOP OF PETAU, A. D. 300

"On the former day [the sixth] we are accustomed to fast rigorously that on the Lord's Day we may go forth to our bread with giving of thanks. And let the parasceve become a rigorous fast lest we should appear to observe any Sabbath with the Jews which Christ Himself, the Lord of the Sabbath, says by His prophets that His soul hateth which Sabbath He in His body abolished."[1]

[1] "Creation of the World," section 4.

Here is another Christian bishop who says most distinctly that Christians did not keep the Jewish Sabbath and that the Lord had abolished it; but they did religiously regard the Lord's Day. This was twenty-one years before Constantine's Sunday law and sixty-four years before the Council of Laodicea.

PETER, BISHOP OF ALEXANDRIA, A. D. 306

"But the Lord's Day we celebrate as a day of joy, because on it He rose again, on which day we have received it for a custom not even to bow the knee" (Canon 15). He gives the same reason for keeping the Lord's Day that Christians give now. This was more than two hundred years before the Pope came into power. Notice that these witnesses for Sunday are from all parts of the world, from Africa, Asia and Europe, not simply from Rome, as Seventh-Day Adventists say. These show that Sunday-keeping was as wide-spread as the Christian Church itself, and that from the earliest days.

EUSEBIUS, A. D. 324

Eusebius was born in Palestine, the very home of Christ and the apostles and the cradle of the early Church. He was Bishop of Cæsarea where Paul abode two years (Acts xxiii. 33; xxiv. 27). He studied at Antioch where Paul labored for years (Acts xv. 1). He travelled to Egypt and over Asia Minor. He was one of the most noted men of his age. He wrote the first history of the Christian Church and bears the title of "Father of Church History." The "Schaff-Herzog Encyclopedia" says: "As a repertory of facts and documents, his work is invaluable." Johnson's "Cyclopedia" says: "He was very eminent for learning, as well as talents." Horne's "Introduction" says: "A man of extraordinary learning, diligence and judgment, and singularly studious in the Scriptures. . . . His chief work is his 'Ecclesiastical History,' in which he records the history of Christianity from its commencement to his own time. . . . He has delivered, not his own private opinion, but the opinion of the Church, the sum of what he had found in the writings of the primitive Christians."[1]

He had every possible opportunity to know what Christians did throughout the world. Of him Justin Edwards, D. D., says: "He lived in the third century, was a man of vast reading, and was as well acquainted with the history of the Church from the days of the apostles as any man of his day." At Cæsarea was "a very extensive library, to which Eusebius had constant access. He was a learned and accurate historian and had the aid of the best helps for acquiring information upon all subjects connected with the Christian Church."[2] He lived right there, knew just what Christians did, and wrote about fifty years before the Council

[1] Vol. I, Chap. xi, Sec. 2, p. 42.
[2] "Sabbath Manual," pp. 124-125.

of Laodicea where Adventists say the Sabbath was changed to Sunday.

True, there was a small heretical sect who kept the Sabbath as Judaizers do now. Of them he says: They are "those who cherish low and mean opinions of Christ. . . . With them the observance of the law was altogether necessary [just like Seventh-Day Adventists] as if they could not be saved only by faith in Christ and a corresponding life. . . . They also observe the Sabbath and other discipline of the Jews just like them, but on the other hand they also celebrate the Lord's Days very much like us in commemoration of His resurrection."[1] Even these Judaizers kept Sunday. On the Ninety-second Psalm he says: "The word by the new covenant translated and transferred the feast of the Sabbath to the morning light and gave us the true rest, viz., the saving Lord's Day." "On this day which is the first of light and of the true Sun, we assemble, after an interval of six days, and celebrate holy and spiritual Sabbaths, *even all nations redeemed by him throughout the world*, and do those things according to the spiritual law which were decreed for the priests to do on the Sabbath." Again: "And all things whatsoever that it was the duty to do on the Sabbath, these we have transferred to the Lord's Day as more honorable than the Jewish Sabbath."[2]

This testimony of the great historian of the early

[1] "Ecclesiastical History," pp. 112-113.
[2] Commentary on Ps. xcii.

Church is decisive. It puts it beyond doubt that Christians in general in all the world did then keep Sunday, the Lord's Day, and did not keep the Jewish Sabbath.

Eusebius bears witness to an actual existing fact, not to some speculative theory. He says that all Christians throughout the world kept the Lord's Day. He lived there and knew of what he affirmed. Is not his testimony better than that of some sectarian Adventist 1,500 years later?

Eusebius says, "We have transferred" the duties of the Sabbath to the Lord's Day. On this Adventists try to make it appear that Eusebius himself with Constantine and others at that date, A. D. 324, were the ones who transferred the day. This is an unfair inference contradicted by all that has gone before. Eusebius writes this as a Christian History relating what the early Church had done. To illustrate: Roosevelt says: "We defeated the British in 1776." "We took Texas from Mexico." Does he mean that *he* and his officers did this now? All know better. Eusebius writes in the same way of what his brethren did centuries before. That is all.

TESTIMONY OF THE COUNCIL OF NICE, A. D. 325

This was the first general council. There were three hundred and eighteen bishops present from all Christendom with about fifteen hundred lower clergy. Surely these would know which day was then observed. The twentieth canon says: "As some kneel on the Lord's Days, and on the days of Pentecost, the holy synod has decided that for the observance of a general rule, all shall offer their prayers to God standing."

There was no objection to this rule, no question about it, all agreed in it as a thing universally understood. The Lord's Day was the Christian day of worship. The Sabbath was not even mentioned, showing that none of them kept it.

As the delegates represented the entire Christian Church and in all nations, it proves that the observance of the Lord's Day was then kept the world over.

ATHANASIUS, A. D. 326

In the great council at Nice A. D. 325, the one man who towered above all others in influence was Athanasius, the "Father of Orthodoxy." There he defeated the heresy of Arianism and settled for the Church ever since the Deity of Christ. He travelled extensively among the Churches, knew their customs well, and was himself a leader among them. It is certain that his teaching and his custom as to the Lord's Day was that of the entire Church. I will quote from the "Seventh-Day Adventist History of the Sabbath," edition 1912, so that his position will not be questioned. The author says: " Of the early Fathers the later ones spare no effort to manufacture new, fanciful, rhetorical phrases to surround Sunday with greater luster, and to cause the Sabbath to fade out of sight. Athanasius of Alexandria (A. D. 326) gives us a fair sample. The sixth psalm is said to be upon the Sheminith (the eighth) an instrument for the eighth key. This is seized upon by Athanasius as a proof for Sunday. "What else could this octave be but the resurrection of Christ?" Then again speaking of Psalm cxviii. 24, "What day can this be but the resurrection day of the Lord?—which has received its name from Him, to wit, the Lord's Day" (pages 418, 419). Then the author gives other quotations from Athanasius along the same line defending the Lord's Day.

Notice that all the great leaders of the Church kept the Lord's Day and defended it, but rejected the Jewish Sabbath. Then did not the general Church follow their leaders? Leaders determine what their Churches believe and practice. Lutherans follow Luther, Methodists follow Wesley, etc. All the leaders of the early Church condemned the Jewish Sabbath and observed the Lord's Day. Did not the Churches follow their teachers then the same as they do now?

Seventh-Day Adventists confess that the leading men, ministers, and writers, during the first centuries opposed the Jewish Sabbath. Thus Elder J. N. Andrews in "History of the Sabbath," edition of 1873, says:

"Several of the early Fathers wrote in opposition to the seventh day. We now give the reasons assigned by each for that opposition.

"The writer called Barnabas did not keep the seventh day" (page 299).

Andrews finds that Barnabas gave *seven* reasons why the Sabbath should not be kept! He wrote A. D. 120, at the very beginning of the second century. His book was read in the Churches as Scripture. Then did those Churches keep the Sabbath? Of course not.

JUSTIN MARTYR, A. D. 140

Of this renowned early Christian Father Andrews says: " He expressly affirms the abolition of both the Sabbath and the Law." " Here are three reasons" (pages 301, 303). So Justin gave his reasons for rejecting the Sabbath. Of him the " Schaff-Herzog Encyclopedia " says: " In these works Justin professes to present the system of doctrine held by all Christians."

IRENÆUS, A. D. 178

Of him Andrews says: " These things indicate that Irenæus was opposed to Sabbath observance " (page 305). He was one of the greatest and most beloved of the early Fathers. Did he oppose the Sabbath and yet all his people keep it? Hardly.

TERTULLIAN, A. D. 200

Of him Andrews says: " Tertullian offers numerous reasons for not observing the Sabbath " (page 305). He not only did not keep it, but gave *numerous* reasons for his faith. Of him Authon's " Classical Dictionary " says: " He informs us more correctly than any other writer respecting the

Christian doctrine of his times." He had a tremendous influence on the Church then. Did they all keep the Sabbath while he opposed it? Reader, how is this?

EUSEBIUS, A. D. 324

No early church Father surpasses Eusebius for learning or influence in the Church.

Of him Andrews says: "Eusebius came out and declared that Christ transferred the Sabbath to Sunday" (page 358). The same "History of the Sabbath," edition of 1912, says: "Eusebius sets aside the Sabbath of the Lord" (page 396). Then that was what all Christians did the world over.

Now if the leaders and representative writers opposed the keeping of the Sabbath, will any one believe that the common Christians all kept a day which all their leaders and writers opposed? Elder Andrews in "History of the Sabbath," page 308, says: "The reasons offered by the early Fathers for neglecting the observance of the Sabbath show conclusively that they had no special light on the subject by reason of living in the first centuries, which we in this latter age do not possess." This is the confession from the ablest historian the seventh day ever had! He admits that "the early Fathers" "in the first centuries" neglected "the observance of the Sabbath and gave their reasons for it!" What further need have we for witness to prove that the seventh day was not observed in the first centuries? But how does this harmonize with the theory that the Sabbath was changed to Sunday by the Pope several hundred years afterwards?

I could multiply indefinitely from Sabbatarian authors such confessions as these. Against their will, they are compelled to make them. They prove conclusively that the observance of the Jewish Sabbath had, largely at least, dropped out of the Church at that early date.

THE COUNCIL OF LAODICEA, A. D. 364

This Christian council plainly states that the Jewish Sabbath was no longer to be kept, while the Lord's Day was. The twenty-ninth canon says: "Christians ought not to Judaize, and to rest in the Sabbath, but to work in that day; but preferring the Lord's Day, should rest, if possible, as Christians. Wherefore if they shall be found to Judaize, let them be accursed from Christ."

Thirty-two bishops were present, all Greeks, in the Eastern Church. Did they know which day the Church kept at that date? Surely. They agree with all the witnesses already quoted. At that date keeping the Jewish Sabbath was condemned, and the Lord's Day approved.

ST. AUGUSTINE, A. D. 395

Next to Paul, probably Augustine has had a wider influence on the Christian Church than any other man. He was born in Numedia, Africa, A. D. 353. His mother was a devout Christian.

He became Bishop of Hippo, Africa. Of him the "Schaff-Herzog Encyclopedia" says: "From his diocese a relentless war was waged upon every heresy." "These made him immortal, and have tempered the theology of all after times." "The Protestants emulate the Romanists in paying him honor." "He claims the reverence of the world." By him "the idea of the Trinity was for the first time clarified."

This great Christian leader, within three hundred years of St. John, had access to all the Christian writings before him, knew perfectly the practice of the Christians in his day the world over and wrote against pagans and every heresy then extant. He explicitly teaches that the Sabbath was not for Christians. Of Sunday he writes often and fully. We quote only a few lines. "That day which we now call Sunday is the first day of the week, as is clearly seen from the Gospels. The first day of the week is thus named as the day of the resurrection of the Lord, by all the four evangelists, and it is known that this is the day which was later called the Lord's Day." "Sunday was not appointed for the Jews, but through the resurrection of the Lord for Christians." "We celebrate the Lord's Day, and Easter, and other Christian festivities." "To fast on the Lord's Day is a great scandal."[1]

Certainly this is plain enough. This brings us down to A. D. 400, with the Lord's Day so fully

[1] To Casulanus, Epistle 28.

and clearly recognized in all Christendom that it is useless to follow it further.

Now read the testimony of the ancient Eastern Greek Church, the first one founded by the apostles. Right Rev. Bishop Raphael, of Brooklyn, N. Y., head of that Church in America, writes me under date of March 30, 1914, as follows: " Our Church, which included all the very first Churches founded by the apostles, such as Jerusalem, Antioch, Ephesus, Corinth, Alexandria, and even Rome, for the first three hundred years, has kept the first day of the week as a day of rest and in holy remembrance of the resurrection of our blessed Lord from the dead. From the dawn of Christianity she bears witness that it has been the sacred day on which the faithful assembled for the partaking of the Lord's Supper, for the saying of public prayers, and the hearing of sermons. All our historians bear record to this fact."

This witness fully confirms the testimony of all the early Christian Fathers quoted in this chapter.

SUMMARY OF TESTIMONY FROM CYCLOPEDIAS

As a fair, impartial and clear statement of the teachings of the early Christian Fathers concerning the observance of Sunday, we refer the reader to the following from Smith's " Dictionary of the Bible," Article " Lord's Day." Here is a book easy of access to all anywhere, unsectarian, embodying the results of the most thorough and scholarly examination of every passage in all the Fathers having any bearing upon the Sunday question. Any one who has read the Fathers must confess that its statements are fair and truthful. I have only room for one short quotation:

"The results of our examination of the principal writers of the two centuries after the death of St. John are as follows: 'The Lord's Day existed during these two centuries as a part and parcel of apostolical, and so of Scriptural Christianity. It was never defended; for it was never impugned, or at least only impugned as were other things received from the apostles. . . . Religiously regarded, it was a day of solemn meeting for the holy eucharist, for united prayer, for instruction, for almsgiving."

So Johnson's "New Universal Cyclopedia," Article "Sabbath," says: "For a time the Jewish converts observed both the seventh day, to which the name Sabbath continued to be given exclusively, and the first day, which came to be called the Lord's Day. . . . Within a century after the death of the last of the apostles we find the observance of the first day of the week, under the name of the Lord's Day, established as a universal custom of the Church."

No higher authority than this could be quoted. It states the truth exactly. So the "Schaff-Herzog Encyclopedia," Article "Sunday," says: "In the second century its observance was universal. . . . The Jewish Christians ceased to observe the Sabbath after the destruction of Jerusalem."

Doctor Schaff, than whom there is no higher authority, says: "The universal and uncontradicted Sunday observance in the second century can only be explained by the fact that it had its roots in apostolic practice."[1]

The man who will shut his eyes to all this mass of testimony and still insist that Sunday-keeping is only an institution of Popes of later ages, is simply held by a theory which he is bound to maintain anyway. I have had a sad experience in this matter, and know just how a seventh-day man feels in reading these historical facts. I read some of them then. They perplexed me some, but I got over this by my strong faith in our doctrines and by believing them to be mostly forgeries. Afterwards as I read more, I saw these testimonies were reliable and very decidedly against our theory of the Pope's Sunday. This disturbed me quite a little, but still I got over them by simply ceasing to think of them at all, and by dwelling upon other arguments in which I had perfect confidence. In debate I was always anxious to shut these out of the discussion. I know that Seventh-Day Adventist ministers generally feel as I did, for we often referred to these testimonies of the Fathers and the effect they had in debate. Of course, the great body of the members never read these things, and are in blissful ignorance concerning them. Or, if they do read them, it is in their own books where they are all explained away. Their unbounded faith in "the message"

"History of the Christian Church," Vol. I, p. 478.

and in their leaders carries them right over these facts as matters of no consequence.

For myself, when once I decided to look these historical facts squarely in the face and give them whatever force they fairly deserved, I soon saw the utter falsity of the claim that the "Pope changed the Sabbath." The old feeling of uneasiness on this point is entirely gone. I feel that so far as the evidence of history is concerned, my feet stand on solid ground.

VII

SUNDAY OBSERVANCE ORIGINATED WITH THE EASTERN, OR GREEK CHURCH, NOT WITH ROME IN THE WEST

THIS is a very important fact bearing on the Sunday question. Adventists are constantly pointing to "Rome," to the "Pope of Rome," to the "Roman Church," to the "Roman Papacy," to the "Roman Councils," and to the "Roman pagans" as the originators of Sunday observance. They publish "Rome's Challenge," "Rome's Catechism," etc. Their cause stands or falls with these claims. It is easy to show that all these assertions are groundless. The change of the day was made in the Eastern Greek Church in the time of the apostles, and was carried thence to Rome, not from Rome to the East. The proof of this is abundant.

Generally people know little about the Greek Church, hardly know that it exists. Yet it is the oldest Church and numbers now one hundred and fifty millions. Generally people suppose that Rome is the "Mother Church," which is not true. As we all know from the book of Acts, the Christian Church began in the East, in Asia, not in Rome. It started in Jerusalem in the East; thence spread over Judea, Samaria, Asia Minor, Greece, Egypt, Damascus, and far-off Babylon on the Euphrates. Rome and the West came later.

Notice briefly: Jesus and all the apostles lived in the East, where the Greek language was spoken. Every book of the New Testament except Matthew was written in Greek. Revelation, written as late as A. D. 96, is in Greek. Largely the preaching of the apostles was in Greek. The Gospel began at Jerusalem in the East (Acts ii. 1–11). Notice who heard that first sermon on Pentecost: " Parthians, and Medes, and Elamites, and the dwellers in Mesopotamia, and Judæa, and Cappadocia, in Pontus, and Asia, Phrygia, and Pamphylia, in Egypt, and in the parts of Libya about Cyrene and strangers from Rome, Jews and proselytes, Cretes and Arabians, we do hear them speak in our tongues the wonderful works of God."

Here were persons from far-off Parthia, Media, and Mesopotamia, away east on the Euphrates, about two thousand miles east of Rome; then come Egypt and Libya; then Arabia; then Asia Minor; then Macedonia; then Crete—all these were in the East. Only one city in the West was named as being represented at Pentecost,—Rome. These first converts carried the Gospel into all these far Eastern countries. The apostles soon followed and raised up Churches there. See where Paul went—Damascus, Arabia, Antioch, Ephesus, Troas, Corinth, Philippi, Galatia,—all Grecian cities. Revelation is written to the seven Churches which are in Asia, none in Rome (Rev. i. 4). Peter's first letter seems to have been from Babylon (1 Pet. v. 13).

Paul was the first minister to visit Rome. This was not till A. D. 65. (See Acts xxviii.) Even then Paul found only a few brethren at Rome, and these were Jews (Acts xxviii.), but no bishop or Pope. For three or four hundred years after Christ the Bishop of Rome had no authority even over a large share of the Churches at home in the West. Over the great Eastern Greek Churches he had none whatever. On the other hand, for about three hundred years the Church at Rome was a Greek mission, supported and ruled over by the Greek Church, as we will soon see.

Long before Paul visited Rome great Churches of thousands had, for half a century, been established in the East, even in far-off nations outside the Roman empire.

Notice another fact. All the first witnesses for the Lord's Day were not Romans, but Greeks living in the East. (See Chapter VI.) These were Barnabas, Justin Martyr, Dionysius, Clement, Anatolius, Origen, Eusebius, etc. Not a single one of the first witnesses for the Lord's Day was a native of Rome. This speaks volumes as to the birthplace of Sunday observance. It was born in the East, not in Rome in the West.

What the Christian world owes to the Eastern, or Greek Church, is thus stated in the "Schaff-Herzog Encyclopedia," Article "Greek Church": "This Church is the oldest in Christendom, and for several centuries she was the chief bearer [missionary] of our religion. She still occupies the sacred territory of primitive Christianity, and claims most of the apostolic sees, as Jerusalem, Antioch, and the Churches founded by Paul and John in Asia Minor and Greece. All the apostles, with the exception of Peter and Paul, labored and died in the East. She produced the first Christian literature, Apologies of the Christian Faith, Refutation of Heretics, Commentaries of the Bible, Sermons, Homilies, and Ascetic Treatises. The great majority of the early Fathers, like the apostles themselves, used the Greek language. Polycarp, Ignatius, Clement of Alexandria, Origen, Eusebius, Athanasius, Basle, Gregory of Nazienzen, Gregory of Nyssia, Chrysostom, Cyril of Jerusalem, Cyril of Alexandria, the first Christian emperors since Constantine the Great, together with a host of martyrs and confessors, belong to the Greek communion. She elaborated the œcumenical dogmas of the Trinity and Christology, and ruled the first seven œcumenical councils which were all held in Constantinople or its immediate neighborhood (Nicæa, Chalcedon, Ephesus). Her palmy period during the first five centuries will ever claim the grateful respect of the whole Christian world."

Notice that the Eastern, or Greek Church, ruled the first seven general councils which were all held in the East, none of them in the West, or papal territory. The date of these seven councils was A. D. 325, 381, 431, 451, 557, 680, and 787. All these were dominated by the Eastern Greek Church, not one by Rome. These take us down this side the latest date Adventists fix for the change of the Sabbath.

Hence, if the Roman Church, or Pope, or Papacy changed the Sabbath, it could only have changed it in the West, for it had no authority or influence over these hundreds of great Greek Churches in the East, many of them outside of Roman rule.

The following is from the Right Rev. Bishop Raphael, head of the Greek Church in America. Few Protestants are aware of the importance and number of that great primitive Church. Read it:

"The official name of our Church is 'The Holy Orthodox-Catholic Apostolic Church.' It was founded in the time of the apostles and by the twelve apostles, Jesus Christ Himself being the Chief Corner Stone, beginning on the Day of Pentecost (Acts ii.). Our Church has never been subject to the Roman Church or to the Latin Popes or to the Papacy. The Roman Church herself was a Greek mission for nearly three hundred years, and the Greek language was the tongue in which the Liturgy, or Mass, was said in the City of Rome.

"The first seven General Councils, beginning with Nice A. D. 325, on down to 787, which were the only General Councils acknowledged alike by Eastern and Western Christendom, were all held within the domain of the four ancient Eastern Patriarchates. They were dominated by the Holy Orthodox-

Catholic Apostolic Church. Even the Popes of Rome, as in the case of Pope Leo in the matter of the exaltation of the Patriarchate of Constantinople to an equality in temporal and spiritual powers, to Rome (vide Acts of the Fourth General Council— Chalcedon), were compelled to assent, like all others, to the Decrees of the General Councils, which latter were always higher than Popes or Patriarchs.

"Rome never dominated any of the first seven General Councils; on the contrary, they dictated to her and in some cases, *e. g.*, Pope Honorius, excommunicated and condemned Popes as heretics.

"The name 'Catholic' was common to all Orthodox Churches, Eastern or Western, Greek or Roman, for eight hundred years after Christ. Rome, in the West, exclusively assumed the name 'Catholic,' yet prefixing it by the appellation 'Roman,' by default on the part of the schismatics within her own patriarchate, in the sixteenth century; but the Holy Orthodox-Catholic Apostolic Church of the East has never from the first been known by any other name than 'Catholic,' nor has she set aside the title in any official document. It is her inalienable property as the Mother Church of Christendom (vide Nicene Creed, Article 9), which, without a single omission, has been from the first proclamation read in our churches. Rome and all Western Christian Churches have never denied to her the title of the 'Mother Church' nor 'Catholic.' Her Apostolicity and Catholicity have been and are acknowledged in all lands and in all ages.

"Our Church, which includes all the very first Churches founded by the apostles, such as Jerusalem, Antioch, Ephesus, Corinth, Alexandria, and even Rome, for the first three hundred years, has kept the 'first day of the week' as a day of rest and in holy remembrance of the Resurrection of our Blessed Lord from the dead. From the dawn of Christianity she bears witness that it has been the Sacred Day on which the faithful assembled for the partaking of the Lord's Supper, for the saying of public prayer, and the hearing of sermons. Our Holy Traditions, the Sub-Apostolic, Anti-Nicene and Sub-Nicene Fathers, as well as all of our historians, also bear testimony to this fact. Under the head of the Fourth Commandment in our Catechism, which is accepted by the whole Holy Orthodox Catholic Apostolic Church, this instruction is given. And both the Roman Church and all other Churches which regard the authority of antiquity, calling themselves Protestant, agree on this very fact, viz., that the Lord's Day (the first day of the week) has been observed from the morning of the Resurrection till this moment.

"The Holy Orthodox-Catholic Apostolic Church consists to-day of not only the four ancient Patriarchates of Constantinople, Alexandria, Antioch, and Jerusalem, but of the great Churches of Russia, Greece, Servia, Bulgaria, Roumania, Montenegro, Albania, Cyprus, Mount Sinai, and the four independent Churches of Austria, etc., and here in America, under the Holy Synod of Russia, a prosperous Mission, consisting of different national Churches, which extends from the northern limits of Canada to the City of Mexico. All these Churches are equal in authority and united in Doctrine, Discipline and Worship. She is the same Church without break, in her succession of bishops, traditions and teaching, from the days of the twelve apostles, when they met in the Upper Room at Jerusalem before there was ever heard of or thought of a Pope in Rome, and when St. James, spoken of as the first Bishop of Jerusalem, presided over the council of the Apostles and Brethren, when they considered the admission of the Gentiles into the Christian Faith.

"The Holy Orthodox-Catholic Apostolic Church has never perceptibly changed in Doctrine, Discipline or Worship since Apostolic Days, and numbers to-day about 150,000,000 members.

"RAPHAEL HAWAWEENY,
Bishop of Brooklyn, and Head of the Syrian Holy Orthodox-Catholic Apostolic Mission in America.
"*March 30, 1914.*"

Their catechism is very plain on this point. The Longer Catechism of the Greek Church says:

"Is the Sabbath kept in the Eastern Church?

"It is not kept strictly speaking.

"How does the Christian Church obey the fourth commandment?

"She still every six days keeps the seventh, only not the last day of the seven days, which is the

SUNDAY OBSERVANCE BEGAN IN THE EAST

Sabbath, but the first day in every week, which is the day of the Resurrection, or Lord's Day.

"Since when do we keep the day of the Resurrection?

"From the very time of Christ's Resurrection."

The catechisms of a Church are the very best authority as to what that Church believes. Here are the Churches raised up by the apostles themselves and have continued this ever since. They have always kept Sunday. Here is a clear and emphatic testimony from the highest authority in that great Eastern Church. All her historians, bishops, councils, catechisms, and traditions agree in witnessing to the observance of the Lord's Day from the very beginning of the Church. This is not a mere *theory*, but an actual historical fact witnessed to to-day by one hundred and fifty million members. And all outside history confirms this.

All the first writers to defend the faith against both pagans and heretics were members of this early Eastern Church. None were Romans. The fundamental doctrines of Christianity now held in common by the Greek, the Roman, and Protestant Churches were first formulated and settled by the Eastern Church, not by the Roman Church. Her great scholars and teachers, her Christian literature, her preachers, and world-wide influence, far exceeded that of Rome and the West for over six hundred years.

Rev. A. H. Lewis, Seventh-Day Baptist, admits that the Greek Church was the Mother Church.

He says: "In the changes of the first four centuries after Christ, the Eastern Church, which was really the Mother Church, and the home of primitive Christianity, was kept unaffected by way of influence which started the strong current of empire westward by way of Rome.—But the truth is that a very large factor of church history is the Eastern current, and especially so in regard to the earliest ideas and practices, that of the Apostolic Period."[1]

This is true, and is an important concession from a Sabbatarian confirming the above from Bishop Raphael. Justin Martyr states in explicit language that as early at least as A. D. 140 that Mother Church was keeping Sunday. (See previous chapter.) How then could Rome, two hundred years later, introduce Sunday to this old Church? How could Sunday originate with the pagan Romans in the time of Constantine, A. D. 321?

It was her apostles and consecrated missionaries who carried the Gospel to Rome and the West and Christianized them. It was not Rome and the West that taught the East. It was exactly the other way. Specially was this true of the observance of the Lord's Day. It was carried from the East to the West, from the Greeks to the Romans. It was not pagan Romans, as Adventists say, who introduced the keeping of the Lord's Day to the great Eastern Church, but it was the Eastern Church that carried that day West and taught the converted pagans to observe it.

[1] "Sabbath and Sunday," pp. 220, 221.

The following is from "The Historians of the History of the World," Article "Papacy," Vol. VIII, p. 520 : "But the history of Latin Christianity was not begun for some considerable (it cannot but be indefinable) part of the first three centuries. The Church of Rome, and most, if not all, the Churches of the West, were, if we may so speak, Greek religious colonies. Their language was Greek, their organization Greek, their Scriptures Greek, and many vestiges and traditions show that their ritual, their liturgy, was Greek. Through Greek the connection of the Churches of Rome and the West was constantly kept up with the East." The "Britannica," Article "Papacy," says that the Church at Rome was not founded till A. D. 41-54. Then it says of the fourth century : "The Roman Church, having ceased to know the Greek language, found itself practically excluded from the world of Greek Christianity." "During the fourth century it is to be noticed that, generally speaking, the Roman Church played a comparatively insignificant part in the West."

These historical facts show that Rome for centuries was taught and ruled by the Eastern Greek Church, not the East by Rome.

The following is from the noted scholar, the late Dean Stanley, Professor of Ecclesiastical History, Oxford, in his "History of the Eastern Church." It is of the highest authority. He says : "By whatever name we call it—'Eastern,' 'Greek,' or 'Orthodox'—it carries us back, more than any other existing institution, to the earliest scenes and times of the Christian religion."[1] "Jerusalem, Antioch, Alexandria, are centers of local interest which none can see or study without emotion, and the Churches which have sprung up in those regions retain the ancient customs of the East, and of the primitive age of Christianity, long after they have died out everywhere else" (page 57).

Again Stanley says : " We know, and it is enough to know, that the Gospel, the original Gospel, *which came from the East*, now rules in the West" (page 95). The Church in far-off Eastern Asia, Chaldea, the home of Abraham, " was the earliest of all Christian missions—the mission of Thaddeus to Agbarus" (page 58). A delegate from that Church came to the Council of Nice, A. D. 325. " The early Roman Church was but a colony of Greek Christians or Grecized Jews. The earliest Fathers in the Western Church, Clement, Irenæus, Hermas, Hippolytus, wrote in Greek. The early Popes were not Italians, *but Greeks*" (page 65).

Consider carefully these facts. It was the Eastern Greek Church which sent missionaries to Rome, founded that Church, furnished it her teachers and supported it as a mission for centuries. For over two hundred years the observance of the Lord's Day was fully and universally established among all the thousands of the old Eastern Churches before the Church at Rome in the West ceased to be taught and supported as a Greek mission. Read

[1] Lecture 7, p. 56.

SUNDAY OBSERVANCE BEGAN IN THE EAST 177

the previous chapter. This shows that Sunday-keeping went from the East to the West, not from Rome to the East. Barnabas, Justin Martyr, and others show that the Greek Churches were all observing the resurrection day in the first part of the second century when they were yet sending teachers and pastors to Rome. Would not these carry their home custom there and teach it to the Roman Church? Certainly, and that is the reason why the West and the East were always agreed about keeping the same day, the Lord's Day. Did that "mission" force on all the old, long established, powerful Eastern Churches a Western Roman pagan day of worship, and that without a word of protest from these Apostolic Churches? Candid men will not accept such an unreasonable assertion.

Again I quote from Dean Stanley. "She [the Eastern Church] is the mother, and Rome the daughter" (page 66). "All the first founders of theology were Easterners. Till the time of Augustine (355-430) no divine had arisen in the West; till the time of Gregory the Great (596-604) none had filled the papal chair. The doctrine of Athanasius [the Trinity] was received, not originated, by Rome" (pages 71, 72). This indicates how dependent Rome was for centuries on the East and how far behind the East Rome was in learning and influence. Again: "There can be no doubt that the civilization of the Eastern Church was far higher than that of the Western" (page 76). "The whole force and learning of early Christianity was in the East. A general council in the West would have been an absurdity. With the exception of the few writers of North Africa, there were no Latin defenders of the faith" (page 100). For over four hundred years the East was the mother, the missionary, the teacher, the leader, the ruler, while the West was the child, the mission, the taught, the led, the one to receive, not give. With the rest of the Gospel the East brought the Lord's Day to Rome and taught it to the less educated Roman.

Here is a notable fact: While the Jewish Christians, and perhaps a few Gentiles living among them, continued for a while to keep the Jewish Sabbath, all Christians, Jews or Gentiles, without a single exception, kept the Lord's Day. Not one single Church in all the early history of the Church has ever been found which did not hold their assemblies on Sunday. Let Adventists name one if they can. They never have, and never can. Another notable fact is: While there was some dispute with a few about the Sabbath, there is not the slightest hint of any dispute among the widely scattered and differing sects of Christians about the Lord's Day. Only one reason can be given for this; namely, the custom of keeping the resurrection day must have begun at the very first with the apostles and was universally accepted by all from the beginning.

Starting out from Jerusalem after Pentecost, the apostles and teachers went everywhere carrying the practice of the Mother Church to all nations.

SUNDAY OBSERVANCE BEGAN IN THE EAST

"The Lord's Day," Rev. i. 10, was thus accepted by all, Rome with the rest.

Here is another great fact. Ignatius, Justin Martyr, Tertullian, and others wrote extensively against all heresies, but not one ever mentioned Sunday observance as a heresy, though it was often mentioned incidentally as a well-known existing Christian practice.

The "Advent History of the Sabbath," edition of 1912, makes this confession: "Although Irenæus writes five books against the heresies, it is rather strange that he himself nowhere alludes to Sunday" (page 334). If the Lord's Day had been a heresy lately introduced from the pagan Romans, he certainly would have named it. His silence is proof that Sunday was not a heretical, pagan institution, for he wrote against all that. Weigh this fact well.

SUMMARY

1. The Eastern Greek Church was first, the Roman Church second and later.

2. The Eastern Church was the mother, the Roman Church the daughter.

3. Christianity went from East to West, not from West to East.

4. The Greek Church was for three hundred years the Missionary Church, while Rome was only the Mission Church.

5. The Greek Church for centuries sent teachers to teach Rome, while Rome never sent teachers to teach the Greek Church.

6. For three hundred years all the great scholars, writers, preachers, leaders, and defenders of the Christian faith were Eastern Greeks, none Western Romans.

7. For six hundred years the learning and scholarship of the Christian Church was in the East, not in the West.

8. For three hundred years the Greek Church furnished the liturgy for the Roman Church.

9. The early Bishops of Rome were Greeks, not Romans.

10. For over five hundred years the Eastern Greek Church far outnumbered the Western, or Roman, Church.

11. For the first eight hundred years all the general councils were held in the East, in Greek territory, were ruled by the Greeks. None by Rome. Rome had to accept these decrees though these councils never recognized the supremacy of the Papacy, but condemned one of the Popes.

12. The Eastern Church has from first to last always opposed and denounced the Papacy of Rome.

13. No Papacy or papal rule has ever had any place in the Eastern Church.

14. The Eastern Greek Church has never accepted a single dogma, doctrine, or practice from the Roman Church—not one. Note this fact.

15. The Eastern Church at the Council of Nice, A. D. 325, formulated the creed of Christendom which Rome accepted at her hands.

16. Rome never claims to have taught Sunday-

SUNDAY OBSERVANCE BEGAN IN THE EAST

keeping to the Eastern Church, though she always claims everything possible.

17. All the thousands of Eastern Churches, composed of millions of Christians, scattered through all nations as far East as India, had been for centuries settled and established in their religious customs before the date when Adventists say Rome introduced Sunday observance from the pagan Romans into the Roman Church.

18. In all church history there is not the remotest reference to any dispute between the Roman Church and the Greek Church about keeping Sunday.

19. The histories, the catechisms, the teaching of her bishops, and her traditions, all agree in teaching in the most positive terms that the Eastern Greek Church has always kept the Lord's Day from the days of the apostles.

20. The Eastern Church strongly asserts that she has kept the Lord's Day from the very beginning.

21. Her catechisms, her historians, and her traditions all confirm this.

22. There is no record of any period in all her history when she did not observe the Lord's Day. Adventist, find it if you can.

23. There is no record showing, or intimating, that she ever received Sunday from Rome or the West.

24. There is no record of any period this side of the apostles when she began keeping the Lord's Day.

25. Justin Martyr, a Greek Christian, a Church Father of the Eastern Church, two hundred years before the date of Constantine's Sunday law, gives a full detailed account of the observance of Sunday by his brother Christians of the Eastern Church.

26. Eusebius, the first church historian, an Eastern Greek bishop of Palestine, before Constantine's law was issued, says, "We have transferred to the Lord's Day all the duties of the Sabbath" (page 153 of this work).

27. The Greek Church, which gave us the Lord's Day, also gave us our New Testament Scriptures long before Rome had any Scriptures in her own tongue.

28. It was the Greek Church which, through her early scholars and councils, gave to all Christendom, Rome included, our canon of inspired New Testament books.

29. The Eastern Church has always jealously held to her own custom against all efforts of Rome to change them.

30. The Roman Catholic Church always teaches that the "Holy Catholic Church" changed the Sabbath in the days of the apostles. (See Chapter IV.) But there was no Roman Pope or Papacy in existence at that time. Even Adventists will admit this. So Rome bears witness that the day was changed in the East, not at Rome. *Mark well this fact.*

31. With all these notorious facts before us, it is absurd to say that Rome changed the Sabbath,

SUNDAY OBSERVANCE BEGAN IN THE EAST

originated the observance of the Lord's Day, and handed it over to the old Eastern Church and then to all Christendom. Such a theory is an utter perversion of all the plainest facts of the history and traditions of the Christian Church.

In the matter of the observance of the Lord's Day, we are not dealing with a mere theory as in the question of election, foreordination, falling from grace, condition of the dead, etc., but with an actual condition, with historical facts.

To-day there are said to be two hundred and fifty million Roman Catholics, one hundred and fifty million Greek Catholics, one hundred and fifty million Protestants, all agreeing in reverencing the Lord's Day, all agreeing that it originated with the apostles. In proof of this all appeal to their present practice, to their entire church history in the past, to all their traditions of their Churches, and to their catechisms. If all this is to be ignored as of no weight, then all the experience and history of all the world is worthless.

FIVE MONUMENTAL WITNESSES OF ALL CHRISTENDOM

To-day we have with us, the world over, five monumental witnesses to the life of Christ, all mentioned in the New Testament.

1. The Church. "I will build My Church" (Matt. xvi. 18).
2. The New Testament Scriptures. "What thou seest write in a book" (Rev. i. 11).

3. Baptism. "Go baptizing them" (Matt. xxviii. 19).

4. The Lord's Supper. "Eat the Lord's Supper" (1 Cor. xi. 19).

5. The Lord's Day. "I was in the spirit on the Lord's Day" (Rev. i. 10).

To-day all Christendom has all five of these in some form; all have come down hand-in-hand together, and one is as old as the other, and each has always been held as sacred as the other, and all have been equally blessed of God.

The Lord's Day is older than some of the New Testament books, its early beginning is better and more clearly attested than most of the New Testament books, especially Hebrews and Revelation.

THE EASTER CONTROVERSY

This question furnishes strong proof that the Lord's Day originated with the beginning of the Church itself, and was universally observed by all Christians from the very first. Of this controversy Dean Stanley says: "It was the most ancient controversy in the Church."[1] It began immediately after the death of the apostles. The "Schaff-Herzog Encyclopedia," Article "Easter," says: "In the early Church there was no uniformity in the day observed." Some Churches celebrated it on the fourteenth day of the Jewish month Nisan, the day of the Passover, no matter what day of the week it came on. The Churches of Syria, Mesopotamia,

---

[1] "History of the Eastern Church," p. 173.

Cilicia, and Asia Minor followed this date. Others celebrated it on the day of the Resurrection, no matter what day of the month it came on. The Eastern Churches of Egypt, Greece, Palestine, Pontus, and the Church of Rome followed this custom. This shows that the apostles felt that it was a matter of indifference and had left no definite instruction about it.

The above named Encyclopedia says: "In the second century this difference was the occasion of a protracted controversy which agitated all Christendom." In A.D. 154 Polycarp visited Rome and tried to reach an agreement but failed. In 197, Victor, Bishop of Rome, threatened to excommunicate those who held to Nisan 15th, but no one obeyed him. Even the Churches in the West paid no regard to his order, while the Eastern Churches condemned and defied him. This shows how little influence the Bishop of Rome had at that date.

This controversy continued to divide and agitate the Church till it was settled by the Council of Nice A.D. 325. The council says: "It has been determined by common consent," indicating that it was not a matter of vital importance either way. Remember that this question was settled by the Eastern Church, not by Rome, for this council was entirely dominated by the East.

Now notice: This simple question as to whether Easter was to be celebrated on a certain day of the month, or on a certain day of the week, divided all Christendom in a hot debate for nearly three hundred years, yet it pertained to only one day in the whole year! Nor did it pertain to more than a few hours' service even in that one day.

Now compare this with the question of the Lord's Day. This came every week during the entire year, fifty-two days, and it embraced the whole day, twenty-four hours every week, yet during all these three hundred years of the early Church there was not one word of division over the observance of the Lord's Day. The question never came up for discussion as to any difference between any parts of the Church, East or West, North or South, Greece or Rome. During the entire Easter controversy the Lord's Day was often mentioned, but only incidentally as an institution well known to all and equally regarded by all, East or West. This uniformity could not have been obtained unless all the apostles had agreed in it and had established it at the very beginning of the Church so that there was no question about it later. Opponents of the Lord's Day have never been able to satisfactorily answer this.

Further, while there were some still who kept the Jewish Sabbath for a while, all these invariably kept the Lord's Day.

No exception to this can be found whether orthodox or heretic. All observe the Lord's Day. Even Sabbatarians are compelled to admit this. Elder Andrews says: "Those Fathers who hallow the Sabbath do generally associate with it the festival called by them the Lord's Day."[1]

[1] "Testimony of the Fathers," p. 11.

Yes, while some did, for a while, keep the Sabbath, yet even they, in every instance, also kept the Lord's Day.

*"I have read this chapter and find it correct.
—BISHOP RAPHAEL."*

Bishop Raphael was educated in three seminaries: Damascus, Constantinople, and Kiev, Russia. He has twice received the degree of "Doctor of Divinity." He is the head of the Greek Orthodox Church in America. Hence, he is well qualified to state correctly the position of the Eastern Church on this question.

VIII

CONSTANTINE'S SUNDAY LAW, A. D. 321

CONSTANTINE, the first Christian emperor of Rome, issued the following edict in A. D. 321:

"Let all the judges and town people, and the occupation of all trades, rest on the venerable day of the sun, but let those who are situated in the country, freely and at full liberty, attend to the business of agriculture; because it often happens that no other day is so fit for sowing corn and planting vines; lest the critical moment being let slip, men should lose the commodities granted by heaven." This law applied only to the Roman Empire. At that date there were numerous Christian Churches outside of the Roman jurisdiction, all keeping Sunday. (See Chapters VI and VII.) This law in no way could affect them. Then where did they get the Lord's Day if this law first introduced it?

Adventists claim that this was a pagan law because it does not use a Christian term, as Lord's Day, or Christian Sabbath. The answer is easy: Christians needed no law to compel them to keep the day, for they all kept it already as a Christian duty. But the pagans kept no weekly day. Hence the law was directed to them, and, of course, used pagan terms for that day, "the day of the sun." That is the manifest explanation of why the pagan name was used. Gibbon says: " Constantine styles the Lord's Day *Dies Solis,* a name which could not offend the ears of his pagan subjects."[1]

Doctor Schaff says: "So long as Christianity was not recognized and protected by the state, the observance of Sunday was purely religious, a strictly voluntary service."[2] "Constantine is the founder, in part at least, of the *civil* observance of Sunday." Before this law all Christians had voluntarily kept the Lord's Day as a religious duty. Now the civil law required pagans to respect the Christian rest day. That is the simple truth and the whole of it. Doctor Schaff, page 380, continues: "Christians and pagans had been accustomed to festival rests; Constantine made these rests to synchronize, and gave the preference to Sunday, on which day Christians from the beginning celebrated the resurrection of their Lord and Saviour. This, and no more, was implied in the famous enactment of 321." The pagan festivals were only yearly, not weekly. Now they were required to keep a weekly rest day on Sunday so as to harmonize with Christians. Adventists now voluntarily kept Saturday as a sacred duty though the civil law does not demand it. Just so Christians voluntarily kept the Lord's Day as a religious duty, though there was no civil law requir-

---

[1] "History of Rome," Chap. xx, Note 8.
[2] "History of the Church," Vol. III, p. 379.

ing it. Now the civil law required pagans also to respect the Christian's day, the day which was then observed by the emperor and all his household.

As to the reliability of Doctor Schaff as a historian, Elder J. H. Waggoner says: "Doctor Schaff is justly esteemed as a man of extensive learning, and whose testimony regarding facts no one will call in question."[1] Good and true. Doctor Schaff says Christians from the beginning voluntarily kept the resurrection day and Constantine made a civil law requiring the pagans to make their festival days harmonize with the established Christian day. *The pagans had to conform to the Christian day, not Christians to the pagan day.*

As we have abundantly proved in Chapter V, the pagan Romans had no weekly festivals. These festivals were all yearly, like our Fourth of July, Thanksgiving, etc. But the Christian's day was weekly, every Sunday. Constantine made these to synchronize. How? "By giving the preference to Sunday," the Christian's day. This is plain enough.

Notice carefully one clause in the decree, viz.: "Those in the country" were to have full liberty to attend to the business of agriculture. Doctor Schaff gives the reason thus: "He expressly exempted the country districts where paganism still prevailed."[2] This is true, and it shows that the pagans did not keep Sunday nor did they wish to. Hence, where they were greatly in the majority,

[1] "Replies to Canright," p. 132.
[2] "Church History," 3d period, Par. 75, p. 379.

they were exempted from obeying this law. But in the cities where Christians largely were, there secular business had to cease. This law was made to protect Christians and the Christian's day, not pagans nor a pagan day. Because Constantine, while yet a pagan with other pagans, reverenced Apollo, the sun-god, Adventists argue that he reverenced Sunday as a sacred day. But this argument is fallacious. Sunday was simply the astrological name of the day, named from the planet, the sun. It had no religious significance whatever, no connection with the worship of Apollo. He was not worshipped on Sunday more than any other week day. That argument is founded on the jingle of words, but not on facts. (See Chapter V.)

The father and mother of Constantine were both Christians, and he venerated them both greatly. His mother was the sainted Helena, one of the most devout Christians of the early centuries. Her influence over her son was always great. Constantine himself thus states the reasons which led him to trust in his father's God, the God of the Christians. "My father revered the Christian God, and uniformly prospered, while the emperors, who worshipped the heathen gods, died a miserable death; therefore, that I may enjoy a happy life and reign, I will imitate the example of my father, and join myself to the cause of the Christians who are growing daily, while the heathen are diminishing."[1] He reasoned thus when made emperor in

[1] Schaff, 3d period, Vol. I, Sect. 2, pp. 19, 20.

A. D. 306. Of him Ridpath says: "He perceived the conclusion of the great syllogism in the logic of events. He saw that destiny was about to write *Finis* at the bottom of the last page of paganism. So, for policy, the emperor began to favor the Christians."[1]

In the year A. D. 312, while on his march towards Rome with his army to meet his enemy, the Emperor Maxentius, he saw, or at least pretended to see, in the heavens, the sign of the cross with the words, "By this conquer." He then adopted that as the banner for his army under which it ever after marched, and always to victory. Here he openly professed conversion to the Christian religion. He immediately issued an edict in favor of the Christians. It has been lost. The "Schaff-Herzog Encyclopedia," Article "Constantine," says: "By the second (Milan 313) he granted them not only free religious worship and their recognition by the state, but also reparation of previously incurred losses. . . . A series of edicts of 315, 316, 319 and 323 completed the revolution." By these edicts paganism was overthrown and finally outlawed from 323. (See the life of Constantine in any history or encyclopedia.)

Adventists unfairly try to place his conversion *after* his Sunday law in A. D. 321. Thus Mrs. White says: "The first public measure enforcing Sunday observance was the law enacted by Constantine two years before his profession of Chris-

[1] "History of the World," Vol. I, Chap. liii, pp. 881, 882.

tianity."[1] This statement alone destroys her claim to inspiration, for it is nine years too late, made with the evident intent to prove his law was pagan. Elder J. H. Waggoner, after naming the decree of 321, says: "At the time when these decrees were issued he had made no profession of Christianity."[2] It is astonishing that a man should put in print a statement so entirely untrue. Nothing is more clearly stated in history than that Constantine openly professed conversion to Christianity nine years before his Sunday edict was issued. (See the life of Constantine by Eusebius.) For years before this he himself and all his household had piously observed the Lord's Day. (See Eusebius, as above.)

The "New Schaff-Herzog Encyclopedia," Article "Constantine," says: "The impression produced by this apparition (the vision of the cross) found its consummation in a dream by night. It is certain from the sources that the decisive conversion of Constantine to Christianity is to be fixed at the outset of the campaign, or in the spring of 312; also that this conversion rested not upon a single experience, the apparition or the dream, but that preparatory experience coöperated with it. . . . Where in passages in Eusebius and elsewhere he speaks of the one religion and belief in one God, he means historical Christianity, and bids, not the Christians, but the pagans, to this doctrine, and in

---

[1] "Great Controversy," edition of 1884, Chap. xxx, p. 391.
[2] "Replies to Canright," p. 29.

this light alone did his Christian and pagan contemporaries understand him."

Here is the clear testimony of an unbiased authority gathered from all the facts in the case which places the professed conversion of the emperor in A. D. 312, just where all reliable historians do. It was nine years before his Sunday law. Dean Stanley[1] places the conversion of Constantine at the same date, 312, right after his vision of the cross. He says: "That some such change, effected by some such means, took place at this crisis, is confirmed not only by the fact of Constantine's adoption of the Christian faith immediately afterwards, but by the specific introduction of the standard of the cross into the army." Gibbon in his "History of Rome," Vol. XI, Chap. XX, p. 184, says: "About five months after the conquest of Italy, the emperor made (A. D. 313) a solemn and authentic declaration of his sentiments by the celebrated edict of Milan which restored peace to the Catholic Church."

From this time on he joined himself with Christians, did all he safely could for them and against paganism till in 323 he outlawed paganism entirely.

The "Encyclopedia Britannica," Article "Constantine," says: "Rome was naturally the stronghold of paganism to which the great majority of the Senate clung with great devotion. Constantine did not wish to do open violence to this sentiment, and therefore resolved to found a new capital."

---

[1] "History of the Eastern Church," Lecture 6, pp. 201, 202.

Stanley relates how the emperor refused to take part in a popular pagan procession in Rome. He openly ridiculed it. Says Stanley, "The Roman people were furious. A riot broke out in the streets." His statue was stoned. This is good proof of his hatred of paganism. His opposition to paganism was his reason for forsaking Rome. He caused his sons to receive a Christian education. Motives of political expediency, however, caused him to delay the full recognition of Christianity as the religion of the state until he became sole ruler of the empire.

Adventists are guilty of misconstruing the plainest intent of that law. They assert that this law compelled pagans and Christians alike to cease work on Sunday, except in the country where both were allowed to work. Then they emphasize the fact that this was the first law ever enacted forbidding work on Sunday. Thus Elder Waggoner says: "It has been fully proved that the decree of Constantine was the first authority for Sunday rest."[1] Yes, certainly, but to whom did this law apply? *To pagans.* It was the first civil law by the state after its head had become Christian. Again Waggoner says: "In the country it *permitted* all to labor, both pagans and Christians."[2] On this it is fair to quote: "A half truth is as bad as a lie." Does that law in any way mention Christians? No. Waggoner assumes that it does, and by this false assumption concludes the Chris-

[1] "Replies to Canright," p. 136.   [2] *Ibid.*, p. 150.

tians worked Sunday, when there is not a hint of such a thing in that law. Our law now permits people to do many things which no Christian will do. At that time Christians reverenced the Lord's Day regardless of what the civil law permitted. Because the law permitted farmers to work Sunday, Adventists assert that Christians worked on Sunday up till that time. They have no proof of this. (See this work, Chapter VI.) For three hundred years it had been a sacred day with Christians. They kept it voluntarily, as Doctor Schaff states above, hence the law in no way applied to them, but it did require pagans, especially in cities where Christians mostly were, to cease work on that day. Constantine, his mother Helena, all his children, his household, his servants, and he himself devoutly observed the Lord's Day at the time this edict was issued, 321. Adventists try to ignore all this to carry their theory that this was a pagan law requiring Christians to reverence a pagan day. It is a bad cause that requires such reasoning.

Another Seventh-Day advocate, Rev. A. H. Lewis, D. D., says: "This edict makes no reference to the day as a Sabbath, as the Lord's Day, or as any way connected with Christianity. Neither is it an edict addressed to Christians."[1] This is a good confession and states the truth exactly. That law was for pagans who had never rested Sundays. This law required them to do what they had never done

---

[1] "Sabbath and Sunday," p. 142.

before—cease work on Sunday. Christians required no such law, for they kept the day as a religious duty without any civil law requiring it. It would have been absurd and useless for Constantine to issue an edict forbidding Christians to work on the Lord's Day when for three hundred years that had been a part of their sacred faith. The very argument Sabbatarians make to prove that this law was addressed to pagans, in pagan terms, is good proof that Christians needed no such law. They kept Sunday voluntarily. Look at the absurdity of the Adventist theory: The pagans were keeping Sunday; Christians were not, but instead were keeping Saturday. Constantine wished all to keep the same day. To whom then would he have addressed his law? To Christians, of course, requiring them to change their day. But he did no such thing; for there was no occasion for it.

Elder J. H. Waggoner makes this confession: "Constantine did nothing whatever that can be construed into changing the Sabbath. In his decrees he said not one word either for or against keeping the Sabbath of the Bible. To this he did not refer in any way."[1] Of course not, for his law was addressed only to pagans who kept neither Saturday nor Sunday. But after his professed conversion in 312, did he not keep pagans in high offices? Did he not order sacrifices to be made to pagan gods? Did he not order some pagan rites to be performed for himself? Yes. Why? Out

[1] "Replies to Canright," pp. 149, 150.

of policy. He had to do so to avoid a rebellion of his pagan subjects who were yet numerous and powerful. He had to bide his time as all wise rulers and reformers do. He could not change the religion and customs of a whole empire in a day. He used common sense, as Lincoln did in abolishing slavery. Lincoln delayed it years after radicals denounced him for his half measures and delay. Now all justify the course he took. Constantine pursued the same wise course in abolishing paganism. So Adventists denounce him as half pagan because he did not play the fool and fanatic and try to do immediately what was impossible. When he first became emperor pagans were in the majority and filled all important offices. He had these to reckon with till he could gradually change all this. By this course he avoided an opposition which would have defeated him. Then he accomplished the religious revolution in a remarkably short time,—ten years. Neither before nor since has the world ever witnessed so tremendous a revolution in so short a period, and his conversion to Christianity did it.

I have before me the "Life of Constantine," by Eusebius, Bishop of Cæsarea, Palestine. He was often with the emperor, in his palace, at his table, in church, in church councils, etc. He related how the emperor, as rapidly as possible, favored Christians and put down paganism, closed their temples, forbade their worship, and wrote and preached against idols.

But Constantine, long after he professed Christianity, retained the heathen title and office of "Pontifix Maximus," or Supreme Pontiff of paganism. Yes, because that still gave him authority to regulate that worship, and he used it to gradually curtail one thing after another in that religion till, in 323, he suppressed it entirely. In this he followed a successful policy, that is all.

In the preceding pages we have clearly proved that Christians had kept Sunday as a sacred day centuries before the time of Constantine. Eusebius, who lived with Constantine, repeatedly says that all Christians were keeping Sunday at that time, and before. We have proved positively, back a few pages, that the pagan Romans did not rest on Sunday, and hence had no Sunday rest day to give to Christians.

Nothing can be more reasonable and simple than the fact that when Constantine professed Christianity he should, as soon as possible, make a law to protect the Christian rest day, the same as Christian rulers have done ever since. That is just what he did do, and that is the whole of it. Whether he was a really converted man, or a mere professor from policy, has no bearing on the question. He *professed* to be a Christian, and all his edicts were issued to favor them, the Sunday law with the rest.

That the law was enacted specially to protect the Lord's Day for Christian worship is distinctly stated by Eusebius in his "Life of Constantine," Chapter

XVIII. Eusebius lived right there where this law was made and when it was made. He was closely associated with Constantine, and has stated clearly why that law was given. Would he not know better than some partisan Adventist sixteen centuries later? Hear Eusebius: "He [Constantine] ordained, too, that one day should be regarded as a special occasion for prayer; I mean that which is truly the first and chief of all, the Day of our Lord and Saviour. The entire care of his household was entrusted to deacons and other ministers consecrated to the service of God, and distinguished for gravity of life and every other virtue; while his trusty body-guard, strong in affection and fidelity to his person, found in their emperor an instructor in the practice of piety, and, like him, held the Lord's salutary day in honor, and performed on that day the devotions which he loved. The same observance was recommended by this blessed prince to all classes of his subjects; his earnest desire being gradually to lead all mankind to the worship of God. Accordingly he enjoined on all the subjects of the Roman Empire to observe the Lord's Day as a day of rest."

Notice that all the servants in Constantine's household were Christians, and all kept the Lord's Day with the emperor. He commanded all his subjects to rest that day so that Christians could be free to attend worship on the Lord's Day. Many Christians were slaves to pagan masters, and could not rest unless their owners did. This law compelled these pagan masters to cease work on that day. Then their slaves could keep the Lord's Day.

Constantine considered himself called of God to care for the Church in external things as the bishops were to care for the internal matters. He said: "You are bishops whose jurisdiction is within the Church. I also am a bishop, ordained by God to overlook whatever is external to the Church."[1] That was why he made his Sunday law—it was to help the Church.

Then there is another reliable witness to the fact that Constantine's Sunday law was to protect the Lord's Day, not a pagan day. The historian Sozomen was born in Palestine, the home of the apostles, only about sixty years after the death of Constantine. He was a noted lawyer in Constantinople, the home of Constantine; hence, was familiar with all the laws of the emperor, and knew their object. Of that Sunday law he says: "He also enjoined the observance of the day termed the Lord's Day, which the Jews call the first day of the week. He honored the Lord's Day, because on it Christ arose from the dead."[2]

This witness by such an authority living right there should be, and is, decisive. That law was to protect the Lord's Day because Christ arose that day, not because it was a pagan festival day. Every candid man must see this. This entirely

---

[1] Eusebius, "Life of Constantine," Chap. xxiv.
[2] "Eccl. Hist.," Chap. ix, p. 22.

explodes the Adventists' theory that it was a pagan law enjoining a pagan day.

Elder A. T. Jones was once the editor of their church paper, and the best posted historian Seventh-Day Adventists ever had. In his recent book, "The Reformation," published in 1913, he not only admits, but truthfully argues, that Constantine's Sunday law was issued at the request of Christians to help the Church. He says: "The Sunday institution and all that was attached to it was wholly of the Church. And when from the federated Church the State accepted and embodied in the law this exclusively church institution, this, in the very fact of the doing of it, was the union of the Church and the State." "It was only in the furtherance of the grand scheme of the bishops and their church-combine to establish the State as 'the Kingdom of God'" (page 375).

Here we have the real truth about that Sunday law. It was issued by a professedly Christian emperor, to favor the Christian Church by protecting their Christian day of worship long held sacred by them. It is readily agreed that the zeal of Constantine to help the Church was unwise and detrimental in its results; but the fact remains just the same.

The edict of Constantine was the very first law ever made by any one prohibiting secular business on Sunday. All historians agree in this. This very fact overthrows the Adventists' claim that the day, as a rest day, originated with the pagans!

Consider now: If these pagan Romans had been keeping Sunday as a sacred day of worship why did they never before have a law forbidding work on that day? Did all these heathens, for ages, cease their work that day voluntarily without any law requiring it? Even in Christian lands, with strict laws against Sunday business, it is difficult to get people to observe the day. Were the heathens more religious than Christians? The Roman emperor was always the head of the pagan religion, the same as the Pope is the head of the Catholic Church. His edict was law to them. He was "Pontifix Maximus," which authorized him to regulate the pagan worship. If it was part of the pagan religion to regard the day as sacred, why is it that the first law prohibiting work on Sunday was never issued till the Roman emperor professed Christianity? I have asked Adventists this question and they make only an evasive answer. The simple fact is this: Up till the time of Constantine Christians were terribly persecuted and were in the minority, and so could make no civil law forbidding work on Sunday, the day they all kept, as we have seen. The pagans did not observe Sunday, but worked that day, the same as on all other days. Hence, they wanted no law to prohibit the work they were all accustomed to do that day. A Sunday law was just what the pagans did not want; hence, he, by his authority as emperor, issued an edict requiring his pagan subjects to rest on Sunday, the same as Christians did and had done for three hundred years. That law was made to favor Christians, not pagans. That this law was made at the request of Christians is admitted by Adventists. Again Elder Jones, in the *Battle Creek Journal*, December 11, 1888, says: "It is demonstrated that the first Sunday law that ever was enacted was at the request of the Church; it was in behalf of the Church, and it was expressly to help the Church."

This truthful admission overthrows the claim that this law was a pagan law to protect a pagan day. It was exactly the opposite—a law to compel pagans to cease work on the day which Christians kept as a sacred day. Put with this the admission of Waggoner above quoted, viz., that "the idea of the rest from worldly labor in its worship was *entirely* new to pagans." So it was, but Christians had kept the day for centuries. With whom, then, "originated" the custom of resting from work on Sunday and keeping it as a sacred day of worship? *It had its origin with Christians, not with pagans.*

IX

THE LORD'S DAY AT THE COUNCILS OF NICE, A. D. 325 AND LAODICEA, A. D. 364

THIS world-renowned council was held at Nice in Grecian territory near Constantinople, A. D. 325. It was the first general council of the Christian Church. Dean Stanley, in his "History of the Eastern Church," devotes one hundred pages to this council. On page 99 he says it was Eastern, held in the center of the Eastern Church. Its decrees were accepted by all Christendom "as a final settlement of the fundamental doctrines of Christianity" (page 102). It was a democratic assembly; no Pope ruled over it (page 107). In calling the council, the Bishop of Rome was not consulted, nor did he or any bishop from Italy attend. Only two presbyters came to represent Rome and only five or six bishops from all the West. There were three hundred and eighteen bishops present. All these were from the Eastern Greek Churches, except the six as above. It was emphatically an Eastern Greek council, held in Greek territory, and conducted in the Greek language. The "Encyclopedia Britannica," Article "Nice," says: "The West was but feebly represented. Two presbyters as deputies of the Roman Bishop, Sylvester, were present. Thus an immense majority of the Synod hailed from the East." McClintock and Strong's "Encyclopedia" says: "Most of the Eastern provinces were strongly represented." Dean Stanley names bishops present "from far up the Nile," from "the interior of Asia," one from Armenia, and one from far-off India.

The "Catholic Encyclopedia" says: "Most of the bishops present were Greeks." It finds only five Western bishops present.

Eusebius in his "Life of Constantine," Chapter VII, names the many countries from whence they came, as "Syrians and Cilicians, Phœnicians and Arabians, delegates from Palestine, and others from Egypt, Thebians and Libyans, with those who came from the region of Mesopotamia. A Persian bishop too was present at this conference, nor was even a Scythian found wanting to the number. Pontus, Galatia, and Pamphylia, Cappadocia, Asia, and Phrygia, furnished the most distinguished prelates, while those who dwelt in the remotest districts of Thrace and Macedonia, of Achaia and Epirus were notwithstanding present. Even from Spain" one came. It will be noticed that this list agrees with the countries named in Acts ii. on Pentecost. Bishops now came from all those countries. Neither Rome nor Italy was even mentioned by Eusebius. As this was a general council of Christendom at that date, 325, it shows how little influence the Roman Church had at that time.

At that date there were one thousand Greek

bishops, representing three million Christians in the East. Doctor Schaff estimates that there were from twelve to fifteen hundred of the lower clergy in that council besides the three hundred and eighteen bishops, or eighteen hundred in all. Of these only six were from the West. The twentieth Article unanimously adopted by that council reads thus: "As some kneel on the Lord's Day and on the days of the Pentecost, the holy synod has decreed that for the observance of a general rule, all should offer their prayers to God standing."

This, it will be seen, simply recognizes the Lord's Day as a well-known Christian day of worship familiar to all that great Eastern council. There was no discussion over it, no opposition to it. Here were eighteen hundred bishops and clergy nearly all from the Eastern Churches. Did any one of them object that they kept the Sabbath instead of the Lord's Day? No, not a hint of it. All were agreed on the day. And this was over a hundred years before the Papacy was born and only four years after Constantine's Sunday law of A. D. 321. Did any of those eighteen hundred ministers of the old established Greek Churches object that the Lord's Day was a new and pagan day which had recently been imposed upon them? Could all Christendom be so quickly and easily changed in so important a matter as that and not a single delegate raise an objection? The simple fact that this great council, so soon after the days of the apostles, should unanimously, without a question, endorse the Lord's Day is proof positive that the observance of the Lord's Day had long been the established custom of the entire Church. The Bishop of Jerusalem, the first Church of all, was there, and voted with the rest. What was said about keeping the Sabbath? Not a word. It is not even mentioned in any way. This shows that it had been dropped very long before this.

An editorial in the *Advent Review and Herald*, February 26, 1914, quotes the following: "I find that three hundred and twenty-five years after Christianity was born, a council of human beings, called the Council of Nice, convened by a human being named Constantine the Great, instituted the first day Sabbath to displace the seventh day Sabbath." The editor endorses this language thus: "The position which the writer of the letter takes is impregnable and the arguments unanswerable."

So according to the *Review*, the editor, and this writer, the first day as the Sabbath was "instituted" here and by this great council! But as we have seen, this was an Eastern council, not a Western one; a Greek council, not a Roman one. Out of three hundred and eighteen bishops present, only six were from the West, or Roman territory, only two presbyters from Rome or Italy. The Churches of Rome, Italy, and the West were of so little account in that great council that Eusebius in his lengthy account of it does not even mention Rome nor Italy! So, then, if the editor and his writer are correct, the Lord's Day was instituted by the Eastern Greek Church, not by the Roman Church, nor by the Pope, nor by the Papacy, for neither had any influence in this council. Their own argument upsets their claim that Rome changed the day.

But, as noted above, this Greek council at Nice, A. D. 325, in no way "instituted" the first day Sabbath to displace the seventh day Sabbath. There is not the slightest hint of such a thing. That is purely an Advent invention, a fair illustration of their groundless assumptions. The Sabbath is not even mentioned. It simply recognized the Lord's Day as a well-known, previously existing institution, and only regulated the attitude in prayer on that day. The change of the day is not even mentioned. It is by such unwarranted statements that the Jewish Sabbath can be defended.

Here, then, were in this august body the most learned and devoted Christian delegates just out from the fires of martyrdom, representing over three million Eastern Greek Christians in Churches founded by the apostles only a short time before. All were unanimous in keeping the Lord's Day. Had the pagans from the then far-off Roman countries brought a pagan day to these devout Greek Churches, and had over three million Greek Christians all immediately given up the old Sabbath and readily accepted this new pagan Roman day without argument or protest? And Adventists ask us to believe all that or be lost!

Now listen to the following from the last edition,

1912, of the "Advent History of the Sabbath": "Both Gnosticism and the council set aside the Sabbath of Jehovah. . . . The emperor and the council showed such aversion to the Sabbath of the Lord" (pages 394, 395).

It makes one sad to read such contradiction of the plainest facts of history. Neither the emperor nor the council so much as mentioned the Sabbath in any way. How then did they show aversion to the Sabbath? Such unwarranted assertions are frequently to be found all through their "History of the Sabbath" and other books.

THE COUNCIL OF LAODICEA, A. D. 364

Over twenty years ago in a widely-circulated article the present writer affirmed that outside of Catholic catechisms, Adventists could produce no proof that the Popes, the Papacy, or the Roman Church changed the Sabbath. Elder J. H. Waggoner, one of their ablest authors, was appointed to the task. Every facility was afforded him. The libraries of America and Europe were searched. As the best he could do he selected the Council of Laodicea, A. D. 364, as the place and time when and where the Sabbath was changed by the Pope. The twenty-ninth canon of that council reads thus: "Christians ought not to Judaize and to rest in the Sabbath, but to work in that day; but preferring the Lord's Day, should rest, if possible, as Christians. Wherefore if they shall be found to Judaize, let them be accursed from Christ."

On this Elder Waggoner says: "Now, if any one can imagine what would be changing the Sabbath, if this is not, I would be extremely happy to learn what it could be." "Now I claim that I have completely met his demand; I have shown the time, the place, and the power that changed the Sabbath."[1] He claims that this was "a Catholic council," and that "historians early and late have made much mention" of this council. Now let us examine his position.

1. If the Sabbath was changed to Sunday by the Pope right here, as he affirms, then certainly it was not changed before nor after nor at any other place. So if this fails their whole cause is lost. Let the reader mark the importance of this fact.

2. He admits what every scholar knows, that till after the time of Constantine the Bishop of Rome had no "authority whatever above the other bishops" and so could not have changed the Sabbath before that time. He says: "It was Constantine himself that laid the foundation of the Papacy."[2] Surely the Papacy did not exist before its foundation was laid.

3. He admits, as already shown, that Constantine did nothing to change the Sabbath.

4. But we have abundantly proved in preceding pages that all Christians long before this date were unanimous in observing the Lord's Day. This one simple fact proves the utter absurdity of

[1] "Replies to Canright," pp. 141, 151.   [2] *Ibid.*, p. 148.

the claim that the Sabbath was changed at Laodicea, A. D. 364, or by the Papacy at any time.

5. In the year 324, or just forty years before the Council of Laodicea, Eusebius, Bishop of Cæsarea, Palestine, wrote his celebrated history of Christianity. He had every possible opportunity to know what Christians did throughout the world. He says: "And all things whatsoever that it was the duty to do on the Sabbath, these we have transferred to the Lord's Day as more honorable than the Jewish Sabbath."[1]

That is the way the Sabbath and Sunday stood in the Church forty years before Laodicea. They did not keep the Sabbath, but did keep the Lord's Day, had transferred all things to it. How much truth, then, can there be in the position that the Sabbath was changed to Sunday by the Pope forty years later?

But let us look at the real facts about the council at Laodicea. Seventh-Day Adventists claim two things, viz.: that the Sabbath was changed by the Roman Church, and that it was done by the authority of the Pope. Then they select the Council of Laodicea as the place and time. But,

1. Laodicea is not Rome. It is situated in Asia Minor over 1,000 miles east of Rome. It was in Asia, not in Europe. It was an Eastern, not a Western town, an Oriental, not a Latin city.

2. It was a Greek, not a Roman city.

3. The Pope of Rome did not attend this council

[1] Quoted in "Sabbath Manual," p. 127.

at Laodicea, A. D. 364. Does Waggoner claim that he did? No, for he knew he did not.

4. The Pope did not attend, nor did he send a legate or a delegate or any one to represent him. In fact, neither the Roman Church nor the Pope had anything to do with the council in any way, shape, or manner. It was held without even their knowledge or consent.

5. At this early date, A. D. 364, the Popes, or rather Bishops of Rome, had no authority over other bishops. It was two hundred years later before they were invested with authority over even the Western Churches. Neither the Pope, nor the Papacy ever had any authority whatever over the Eastern Churches where this little council was held. (See Bower's "History of the Popes," or any church history.) Speaking of Sylvester, who was Bishop of Rome A. D. 314 to 336, only twenty-eight years before this council at Laodicea, Elder Waggoner says: "The Bishop of Rome had not then yet attained to any authority whatever above the other bishops."[1] This is true. Did they in the next twenty-eight years gain authority to change the keeping of the Sabbath from one day to another throughout the whole world? Preposterous!

6. Liberius was Bishop of Rome at the time of this council at Laodicea. He was degraded from his office, banished, and treated with the utmost contempt. Bower says that in order to end his

[1] "Replies to Canright," p. 143.

exile, Liberius "wrote in a most submissive and cringing style to the Eastern bishops."[1] And this was the Pope who changed the Sabbath at a council of these same Eastern bishops, 1,000 miles away, which he never attended!

7. The Council of Laodicea was only a local council, a small, unimportant affair and not a general council at all. Elder Waggoner magnifies it into a great "Catholic [general] council," a claim which is utterly false. The general councils are: 1. That at Nice, A. D. 325. 2. That at Constantinople, A. D. 381. 3. That at Ephesus, A. D. 431, etc. (See Chapter VIII of this work, p. 188. See also the list in Johnson's "Cyclopedia," or any ecclesiastical history.) Bower in his extensive work, the "History of the Popes," gives an account of all the general councils, the important local councils, and all with which Rome or the Popes had to do, but does not even mention this one at Laodicea. He mentions many councils held about that time, but not this one. He says: "Several other councils were held from the year 363 to 368, of which we have no particular account."[2]

8. I have searched through a number of cyclopedias and church histories and can find no mention at all of the council at Laodicea in most of them, and only a few lines in any. Doctor Schaff, in his "History of the Church," gives an extended account of all the general councils, but makes

[1] "History of the Popes," Vol. I, p. 64.
[2] Vol. I, p. 79.

no mention of Laodicea. Rev. W. Armstrong, a scholar of Canton, Pa., says: "This council is not even mentioned by Mosheim, Milner, Ruter, Reeves, Socrates, Sozomen, nor by four other historians on my table." McClintock and Strong's "Cyclopedia" says of this council: "Thirty-two bishops were present from different provinces in Asia." All bishops of the Eastern Church, not one from the Roman Church! And yet this was the time and place when and where, according to Adventists' views, the Roman Church and the Pope changed the Sabbath! At that date there were about two thousand bishops and eight million Christians scattered all over the world.

9. Now think of it: this little local council of thirty-two bishops revolutionizes the whole world on the keeping of the Sabbath immediately without opposition!

10. The fact is that this council simply regulated in this locality an already long established institution, the Lord's Day, just the same as council after council did afterwards. If this changed the Sabbath to Sunday, then it has been changed a hundred times since! Sabbatarians point to these different regulations as so many acts in changing the Sabbath, when they have not the remotest relation to such a thing any more than have the resolutions with regard to keeping Sunday which are passed year by year now in all our religious assemblies. Elder E. J. Waggoner makes this truthful statement: "The decrees of councils have not as a gen-

eral thing been arbitrary laws telling what *must be*, so much so as they have been the formulation of the opinions and practices largely prevalent at the time. . . . Infallibility had been attributed to the Pope hundreds of years before it became a dogma of the Church."[1] Exactly, and just so the Lord's Day had been kept by the Church hundreds of years before the Council of Laodicea mentioned it.

11. The Church of Laodicea where this council was held was raised up by Paul himself (Col. iv. 13, 16; 1 Tim. vi., close of the epistle). It was one of the seven Churches to which John wrote (Rev. iii. 14). Hence it is certain it was well instructed and grounded in the doctrines of the apostles. Between Paul and this council, that is A. D. 270, Anatolius was Bishop of Laodicea. He wrote: "Our regard for the Lord's resurrection, which took place on the Lord's Day, will lead us to celebrate it on the same principle" (Canon 16). Here we have that Church keeping Sunday one hundred years before this council.

12. Finally, if the Council of Laodicea changed the Sabbath, as Adventists say, then it was changed by the Greek Church instead of the Roman Church; changed by the Eastern Churches over which Rome had no authority; changed before the Papacy was established, by a small local council which neither the Pope nor any of his servants attended. The absurdity of this claim is manifest without further argument.

---

[1] "Fathers of the Catholic Church," p. 333.

But what did that council do about the Sabbath anyway? It says Christians should not Judaize by keeping the Sabbath, but should keep the Lord's Day. What occasioned this reproof? Eusebius, the first church historian, writing forty years before, has this in Chapter XXVII:

"THE HERESY OF THE EBIONITES

"They also observe the Sabbath and other discipline of the Jews, just like them, but on the other hand, they also celebrate the Lord's Day very much like us, in commemoration of the Resurrection."

In his "History of the Church," Eusebius gives the doctrines and practices of the great Christian Church at that time, which then numbered five million. But there was a little heretical sect called Ebionites. What was their error? Wherein did they differ from the universal Church? They insisted on keeping the Jewish Sabbath together with the Lord's Day. So then, forty years before Laodicea, keeping the seventh day was branded by all the Church as a heresy, just the same as it is now. It was practiced only by a few, and this council condemned it. The Eastern Greek Church was the one that here put down the observance of the Jewish Sabbath, that is, if this was the time and place when it was done. What, then, becomes of the assertion that the change of the Sabbath was made by the Pope, the Papacy, or the Roman Church?

Now when Elder Waggoner rested his case on the Council of Laodicea as the time and place when and where the Sabbath was changed, did he not fail and fail utterly? As seen above, that was a council of Eastern bishops, a Greek council, which neither the Pope nor any one to represent him attended. Neither the Pope, nor the Papacy, nor the Roman Church had the remotest thing to do with it. As well claim that Russia established our Fourth of July. In Waggoner's failure, the denomination failed, for he was chosen to defend them on this vital point.

X

THE PAPACY AND THE LORD'S DAY

"THE Papacy changed the Sabbath."[1] This is a leading tenet in the Seventh-Day Adventist faith, strongly urged in all their teachings. Here is a sample in their own words from "Words of Truth," Series No. 33: "They believe that the change of the Sabbath from the seventh day to the first day of the week was brought about by the Papacy, and that this change of the Sabbath is foretold in prophecy (Dan. vii. 25), and that it constitutes the sign, or mark of the Papacy." All their literature, specially that of Mrs. White's, abounds in these strong assertions.

Nothing could be farther from the truth than this claim. All history is against it.

It should be carefully understood that the Papacy is distinctly and wholly a product of the local Church at Rome, the Latin Church, the Church in the west, in Italy. The "Papacy," in no sense of the word, began to exist at the very earliest till four or five centuries after Christ. At first it was confined entirely to Italy, then was gradually extended over the Western Churches. It was not fairly established even there till A. D. 600. It

[1] "Replies to Canright," p. 119.

never was recognized in the East by the great Eastern Greek Church, not even up to this day. The "Schaff-Herzog Encyclopedia," Article "Papacy," says: "During the first period after the foundation of the Christian Church, the Bishops of Rome exercised no primacy. The Council of Nice (325) knows nothing of a primacy of Rome over the rest of the Church." This is well into the fourth century.

Johnson's "New Universal Cyclopædia," Article "Pope," says: "No supremacy was either claimed or recognized during the first, second, and third centuries, and when, in 343, at the Council of Sardica, the supremacy of the Roman see over the Christian Church was spoken of for the first time in undisguised terms, the Oriental (Eastern) bishops protested and left the council." This is near the middle of the fourth century again, but even here it was opposed and that council was never recognized in the East.

But Adventist authorities themselves will settle this point. Elder J. H. Waggoner says: "Sylvester was Bishop of Rome during the most of the reign of Constantine [312–336]. He decreed that Sunday should be called the Lord's Day. [There is no such decree. D. M. C.] But this could affect the Church of Rome only, for the Bishop of Rome had not then yet attained to any authority whatever above the other bishops." "It was Constantine himself who laid the foundation of the Papacy."[1]

[1] "Replies to Canright," pp. 143, 148.

THE PAPACY AND THE LORD'S DAY

Elder Waggoner admits what history abundantly proves, namely, that up to the fourth century the Bishop of Rome had no authority over other bishops, and that the foundation of the Papacy was not laid till A. D. 325 at the Council of Nice. Certainly then the Papacy did not exist before the foundation for it was laid. But, in Chapter VI of this book, we have given plenty of proof that Sunday was observed by all Christians as early, at least, as A. D. 140, or nearly two hundred years before even the foundation of the Papacy was laid, as Waggoner admits. Turn back to page 137 and read where Justin Martyr says: "On the day called Sunday, all who live in cities or in the country gather together to one place," and then describes their meetings nearly the same as we conduct them now. Again he says: "But Sunday is the day on which we *all* hold our common assembly," etc. Here we have Sunday observed by all Christians two hundred years before the Papacy existed, before the Bishop of Rome could exercise authority over other bishops. This shows the folly of attributing the beginning of Sunday-keeping to the Papacy two hundred years later.

Coming down still further to the middle of the fifth century, Waggoner quotes with approval the following from McClintock and Strong's "Cyclopedia":

"Leo I, saint and Pope, surnamed the Great, noted as the real founder of the Papacy."

This was as late as the middle of the fifth

century. In the same article McClintock and Strong say of Leo's attempt to rule other Churches: "A strong opposition was speedily organized both in the West and in the East, and soon assumed the attitude of open defiance." Only a small part of even the West paid any heed to Leo's claims. The East defied him. How much influence could the Papacy at that date have in changing the Sabbath the world over? None at all. The Catholic monthly, *The Ecclesiastical Review*, February, 1914, page 237, speaking of the controversy over Easter, A. D. 154, says: "Shy then, as it always has been, of introducing Western observances, the Eastern Church sent St. Polycarp to Rome" to protest against this meddling with the Eastern custom. As this Catholic author admits, that has always been the attitude of the Eastern Greek Church towards Rome—the attitude of opposition. How, then, could the Papacy impose on those great independent Eastern Churches a pagan day which they had never kept? Adventists take their stand at the Council of Laodicea, A. D. 364, and claim that the Sabbath was changed there. Of the decree of this council Waggoner says: "I have shown the time, the place, and the power that changed the Sabbath."[1]

Here is his proof that the Papacy changed the Sabbath and he stakes all upon it. But in Chapter IX we have shown that this was an Eastern Greek council, held in Greek territory, Asia Minor,

[1] "Replies to Canright," p. 151.

by the Greek Church, attended only by Greek bishops. Not one single person was there from the Roman, or Latin, Church in the West. Neither Pope nor Papacy had the slightest thing to do with it. Hence, the attempt to prove that the Papacy changed the Sabbath here is a failure. Moreover, neither Pope nor Papacy yet existed. The Bishop of Rome at that time had no authority over other bishops of equal rank with himself of which there were many.

The Papacy was entirely a Roman affair, limited for centuries to Italy, then gradually gaining influence over the Western Churches. But in the East, among the millions of Greek Christians, who for centuries were far greater in number, intelligence, and influence, any such thing as a Papacy was wholly unknown. There no one centralized authority has to this day ever been acknowledged. Four patriarchs of equal authority nominally govern there. These are in Constantinople, Antioch, Jerusalem, and Alexandria. In the fourth, fifth, and sixth centuries when the Roman Papacy undertook to claim some jurisdiction there, it was hotly resented by all the Eastern Churches. The opposition between these two great sections of the Church grew with increasing bitterness till A. D. 1052, when the East excommunicated Rome because it would never acknowledge any authority of the Roman Papacy. They are separate now. The Greek Church now claims a membership of about one hundred and fifty million. With the

Protestant Churches, who number over one hundred and fifty million and who all repudiate the Papacy, one-half, or more, of all Christendom is outside the Roman Papacy and opposed to it. So it must be remembered that the Roman Catholic Church, or the Papacy, or the Pope, has never had rule over more than a divided part of the Christian Churches. Yet all the Churches which were never subject to Rome keep Sunday and always have. This proves that Sunday observance did not come from Rome.

Another very important fact is to be noticed here; namely, that in the first four centuries during which the observance of the Lord's Day was fully settled in all Christendom, the Roman Church was greatly in the minority both in numbers, in great Christian leaders, in learning, and in influence.

Here is another fact: All the fundamental doctrines of orthodox Churches, whether Protestant, Papal, or Greek, were first wrought out and settled in their present form by the Eastern Greek Christian scholars, church leaders, and œcumenical councils dominated by the Eastern Church. These include the canon of our Holy Scriptures, the deity of Christ, the Trinity, the passing of the Jewish Sabbath, the observance of the Lord's Day, etc. The Papal Church accepted all these from the Eastern Church and later endorsed them, but originated none of them. This cuts up by the roots the Advent theory that Sunday-keeping originated with the Papacy.

THE PAPACY AND THE LORD'S DAY

The Greek General Council, 680, excommunicated Pope Honorius. On this the "Schaff-Herzog Cyclopedia," Article "Councils," says: "A fact rather embarrassing to the dogma of papal infallibility." This shows what little influence the Popes or Papacy had as late as 680, and how little attention the Greek Church paid to Rome. Schaff's "History of the Church," Vol. III, p. 325, says: It consisted of five hundred and twenty bishops, only five of whom were from the Western or Roman Church; all the rest were Greeks and Orientals, and that is the date when Leo I was Bishop of Rome, the one who is said to be the first founder of the Papacy. It shows how little influence in the great councils of the Church that infant had then.

Stanley says: "The Council of Constantinople was avowedly only an Eastern assembly; not a single Western bishop was present."[1] Yet this was a general council and accepted by Rome.

But according to the arguments of the Adventists themselves, the Sabbath was changed by the Greek council at Laodicea, A. D. 364, eighty-seven years before the Papacy was so much as founded! In view of the above facts what becomes of the assertion that the Sabbath was changed by the Papacy? Adventists cannot produce a single witness saying that the Papacy changed the Sabbath. Yet it is the main prop of their theory.

The arguments of the Adventists themselves put together overthrow their own position. Thus of

[1] "Hist. East. Ch.," p. 102.

the year A. D. 300, their "History of the Sabbath," pp. 373, 374, edition of 1912, says: "We have now followed the history of Sunday from the time it was first mentioned by the Gnostic Pseudo-Barnabas, A. D. 120, as the mysterious eighth day, until it stands out clearly and definitely as the first day of the week called the Lord's Day." Here then, A. D. 300, it was clearly and definitely "the Lord's Day." This they have admitted. Coming to the Council of Nice, A. D. 325, the *Advent Review*, February 26, 1914, says: "The Council of Nice instituted the first day Sabbath to displace the seventh day Sabbath." So here as early as A. D. 325, they have the Sabbath changed by this great Eastern Greek council.

So their "History of the Sabbath," edition of 1912, of this council says: "By this Canon 20, the council set its seal upon the Sunday law of Constantine passed by the State. Henceforth Sunday was not only the legal holiday of the State, but its observance was acknowledged and regulated by the action of the first general council of the Church." "Thus the highest civil and ecclesiastical authorities enforced Sunday as the universal, legal weekly holiday for all the subjects of the vast empire" (page 406). All right. Now if the observance of Sunday was thus firmly established both by the State and the Church, A. D. 325, was not its observance settled forever? Surely. How then could the day be changed by the Papacy which was not founded till over a hundred years later?

And if the change of the Sabbath was made and settled both by the Church and the State in all the vast empire A. D. 325, how could the Sabbath be changed again at Laodicea A. D. 364, about forty years later?

Their various and contradictory theories eat each other up. As we have seen both the Encyclopedia and Waggoner agree that Leo was the real founder of the Papacy. But, as above, Waggoner himself definitely locates the change of the Sabbath in A. D. 364, or at least seventy-six years before the founder of the Papacy came into office!

But when was the Papacy really established? Adventists themselves locate it in A. D. 528. Smith, in "Thoughts on Daniel and Revelation," on Dan. vii. 25, says: Justinian "issued that memorable decree which was to constitute the Pope the head of all the Churches, and from the carrying out of which in 538 the period of papal supremacy is to be dated." This was in the sixth century. That great work, Bower's "History of the Popes,"[1] locates the establishment of the Papacy in A. D. 600.

For two hundred years previous to this the Bishop of Constantinople had held the title of "universal head of the Catholic Church." It had been confirmed to him by emperors and a great council. (See Bower as above, same page.) Dowling's "History of Romanism" is another high authority on this subject. On page 39 read: "The papal supremacy not established in the fourth century."

[1] Vol. I, pp. 426, 427.

On page 41 he says that the Council of Chalcedon (451 A. D.) decreed the equality of the Bishops of Rome and Constantinople. The great patriarchs of Antioch and Alexandria were made subject to the Bishop of Constantinople who was thus greater than the Bishop of Rome and opposed him bitterly. On page 51 Dowling says: "During the last few years of the sixth century, the contest for supremacy between the Bishops of Rome and Constantinople raged with greater acrimony than at any previous period. The Bishop of Constantinople not only claimed an unrivalled sovereignty over the Eastern Churches, but also maintained that his Church was, in point of dignity, no way inferior to that of Rome." It will be seen that Rome had no influence over the Eastern Churches, and hence could not have effected any change in their day of worship if it had tried.

Is there any statement anywhere in any history that the Pope or the Papacy ever tried to change the keeping of the day in the Eastern Church? There is not the remotest hint of such a thing. Roman Catholics never mention it, never claim it. It is useless to follow the history of the Lord's Day this side of Laodicea, A. D. 364, for even Adventists admit that the change of the day had been made by that time. All agree, and Adventists admit, that the Papacy was not formed till after this— long after. So the Papacy could not have changed the Sabbath when it had already been changed hundreds of years before there was any Papacy.

THE PAPACY AND THE LORD'S DAY

But Adventists try to get over this difficulty this way: They say "The *spirit* of the Papacy existed ages before the actual founding of the Papacy occurred." Answer: What is the spirit of the Papacy? It is to centralize all authority of Church and State in one person, the Pope of Rome. Then this centralizing, one-man, autocratic personage, with despotic power, crushes out all opposition to his will. This is the spirit of the Papacy. But in the great Eastern Church composing the great majority of Christendom for four or five hundred years, there was from the very beginning a deadly opposition to any such spirit of centralized authority. To this day it has never been tolerated there. From the first council in Jerusalem (Acts xv.) to the present a democratic spirit has existed and has been dominant there. Stanley says: "A similar turn is given to the institution of the Eastern clergy by the absence of the organizing, centralizing tendency which prevailed in the West."[1] Again: "The centralization of the West, as displayed in the Papacy, is unknown in the East" (page 85). Again: "The Eastern patriarchs speak in their solemn documents of the papal supremacy as the chief heresy of the latter days" (page 90).

There was never any Papacy or spirit of Papacy in the Eastern Church, or any recognition of the Roman Papacy, but a bitter hostile opposition to it till finally it caused a separation of the two in 1052. Hence, "the Spirit of the Papacy" never has ex-

[1] "History of the Eastern Church," p. 83.

isted in the Eastern Church where the Sabbath was changed.

Specially mark this fact: The observance and sanctity of the Lord's Day was fully established throughout all the great Eastern Churches long before the Roman Papacy could rule even in the West, much less in the East.

Adventists make this mistake: Beginning right after the apostles, wherever they find Christians falling into false notions or heretical doctrines, or adopting worldly ways, they pronounce that "the spirit of the Papacy." All their books on the history of the Sabbath and Sunday are largely made up of this kind of argument. But it is a fallacy. At present we have numerous Churches which are neither orthodox nor evangelical, such as Universalists, Unitarians, Christian Scientists, Swedenborgians, etc. But none of these have any of the spirit of the Papacy. So we have many worldly Christians and worldly churches, but they do not favor any Papacy.

So in the early centuries, those in the Eastern Church who fell away from the faith, or lapsed into worldliness, did not thus become papists, nor have the spirit of the Papacy. The Papacy, from its very earliest inception to its full establishment, was entirely of the local Church at Rome and the bishops of that Church. Because it was the imperial city, these bishops finally became ambitious to rule over other Churches. They schemed and worked till after long centuries they gradually subdued Church after Church, bishop after bishop, and see after see, till about A. D. 600 the Roman Papacy was established in the West, but never in the East.

The "spirit of the Papacy" was born at Rome in the Bishops of Rome and was wholly confined to the Roman Catholic Church in the West. It was never tolerated in the Eastern Church, nor has it ever had the slightest thing to do with the Sabbath question there. But the Lord's Day was firmly established in all Christendom, East and West, centuries before the Papacy succeeded in establishing itself even in Rome. Hence it is utterly false, absurd, and contrary to the plainest statements of all history to claim that the Lord's Day originated with the Papacy at Rome, and was then forced on the great Eastern Churches over which the Papacy never had any authority.

"I have read this chapter and find it correct.
—BISHOP RAPHAEL."

Bishop Raphael was educated in three seminaries: Damascus, Constantinople, and Kiev, Russia. He has twice received the degree of "Doctor of Divinity." He is the head of the Greek Orthodox Church in America. Hence, he is well qualified to state correctly the position of the Eastern Church on this question.

XI

THE MARK OF THE BEAST—WHAT IS IT?

SEVENTH-DAY ADVENTISTS teach that the ten-horned beast of Rev. xiii. 1–10 is the Papacy and that the two-horned beast of verses 11–18 is the United States. No commentator or Christian scholar of this or any other age of the Church agrees with them in this. Plausible expositions of these symbols have been offered, many of them far better sustained than the one Adventists have invented. For myself, I am sure they are wrong on both these beasts, but I will not argue that point as it is not essential in the question before us. Grant their claim that the beast is the Papacy, then the question is, What is the supreme mark of the Papacy? This is easily settled.

1. *Seventh-Day Adventists* assert in the most positive manner that the Pope changed the Sabbath to Sunday. "The Pope has changed the day of rest from the seventh to the first day."[1]

2. Then they affirm that "Sunday-keeping must be the mark of the beast."[2] "The Sunday Sabbath is purely a child of the Papacy. It is the mark of the beast."[3] "Sunday the distinctive mark of

---

[1] Mrs. White, "Early Writings," p. 55.
[2] "The Marvel of Nations," by U. Smith, p. 183.
[3] *Advent Review*, Vol. I, No. 2. August, 1850.

papal power." This is the heading of Chapter XXII in their "History of the Sabbath," 1912. The whole chapter is devoted to it. They thunder this into the ears of people, and threaten them with God's wrath if they keep Sunday, till they frighten ignorant souls to give it up.

3. This change in the Sabbath, they say, was made by the Popes at the Council of Laodicea, A. D. 364.[1] This was over 1,500 years ago.

4. All who keep Sunday, they assert, worship the beast and receive his mark. "Sunday-keeping is an institution of the first beast, and *all* who submit to obey this institution emphatically worship the first beast and receive his mark, 'the mark of the beast.' . . . Those who worship the beast and his image by observing the first day are certainly idolaters, as were the worshippers of the golden calf."[2] This language is too plain to be mistaken. All who keep Sunday are idolaters and have the mark of the beast.

5. But, strange to tell, they now all deny that any one has ever had the mark of the beast. "We have never so held," says Smith.[3] All right, though this is a square denial of what they once taught, as above. It is a common thing for them to change their positions and then deny it. We proceed:

6. The United States will soon pass a strict

---

[1] "Replies to Elder Canright," p. 151.
[2] *Advent Review Extra*, pp. 10 and 11, August, 1850.
[3] "Marvel of Nations," p. 184.

Sunday law and unite Church and State; then all who still keep Sunday will have the mark.[1]

ANSWER

Does the Bible say that the mark of the beast is keeping Sunday? No, indeed. That is only another one of their assumptions. To establish this, they have to make a long, roundabout set of arguments, built upon inferences none of which are sound. Their theory is false, because:

1. The Jewish Sabbath was abolished at the cross (Col. ii. 16). Hence, it was not changed by the Pope.

2. Sunday is the Lord's day of Rev. i. 10. (See Chapter VI of this book.)

3. The Pope never changed the Sabbath. This point I have proved conclusively. This fact alone upsets their whole argument on the mark of the beast.

THE ABSURDITIES OF THEIR POSITION

1. Sunday-keeping has been the mark of the beast for 1,500 years. During all this long time millions have kept Sunday on the sole authority of the Roman Church, and yet no one had the mark!

2. The keeping of Sunday has been time and again and in many countries enforced by law and severe penalties, just as they say it will be in the future here, and yet none of those who have kept it as thus enforced have had the mark of the beast!

---

[1] "Marvel of Nations," p. 185.

3. Church and State have been united in various countries, and have enforced this institution of the Papacy, as they call it, and yet it was not enforcing the mark of the beast!

4. For over 1,500 years, taking their own dates, all the pious of the earth, the martyrs, the reformers, the Luthers, Wesleys and Judsons, have observed Sunday and enjoyed the blessing of God, but now, all at once, the whole world, Christians and all, are to be damned and drink the wrath of God for doing just what all holy men have done for ages! Of Sunday-keeping in the future, Mrs. White says: "That must be a terrible sin which calls down the wrath of God unmingled with mercy."[1] This terrible sin is just what all the Church of Christ has practiced for ages, and yet have had God's blessing! How absurd.

5. It is attempted to dodge this point by saying that those of other ages did not have the light on the Sabbath. This is not true. Luther, Bunyan, Baxter, Milton, all had the "light" on the Sabbath question, and rejected it and wrote against it. Then I can do it, too, and not have the mark of the beast, if they did not.

6. If it is worshipping the beast to rest from physical labor on Sunday after one knows that Sunday is the Pope's Sabbath, then many Seventh-Day Adventists are worshippers of the beast. Why? Because they often rest on Sunday. Book agents, colporteurs, teachers, drummers, per-

[1] "Great Controversy," p. 282.

sons visiting relatives, ministers in new places, etc., all frequently rest on Sunday, and even go to church and hold meetings all day! Are they worshippers of the beast? Why not? Do you say they only do it for convenience or from policy? Just so they can rest on Sunday for the same reason when the law shall require it, and not worship the beast any more than Adventists do now.

7. Deny it as they may, the Seventh-Day Adventist teachings do make all Sunday-keepers, both now and in past ages, worshippers of the beast, having the mark of the beast. Here is proof in their own words:

1. The Pope changed the Sabbath. Sunday is only the Pope's day. (See above.)

2. "The mark of the beast is the change the beast made in the law of God" in the Sabbath.[1] Then the mark of the beast existed as soon as the change was made, which they locate 1,500 years ago. Is not this conclusion inevitable? If the mark of the beast is the change of the Sabbath which was made by the Papacy in the fourth century, then that mark has existed ever since. There is no escape from this conclusion.

3. All who have kept the law since that date, as changed by the beast, have been keeping the law of the beast, not the law of God; have been worshippers of the beast, not worshippers of God. Here is their own argument for it: Referring to the prophecy that the Papacy should "change

[1] "Marvel of Nations," p. 175.

times and laws" (Dan. vii. 25), which they claim the Pope fulfilled A. D. 364 by changing the Sabbath to Sunday, Elder Smith says: "When this is done [which is 1,500 years ago], what do the people of the world have? They have two laws demanding obedience"—the law of God and the law of the Pope. "If they keep the law of God, as given by Him, they worship and obey God. If they keep the law as changed by the Papacy, they worship that power. . . . For instance, if God says that the seventh day is the Sabbath, on which we must rest, but the Pope says that the first day is the Sabbath, and that we should keep this day, and not the seventh, *then whoever* observes that precept as originally given by God, is thereby distinguished as a worshipper of God; and he who keeps it as changed is *thereby marked* as a follower of the power that made the change. . . . From this conclusion no candid mind can dissent."[1]

Then, for the past fifteen hundred years, all who have kept Sunday have been "marked" as followers of the beast and have worshipped him! From their own argument, does not this inevitably follow? Of course it does. When they try to deny and evade this conclusion, they simply contradict and stultify themselves. Either their argument is a fallacy, or else this conclusion must follow. Look at this hideous Moloch which they have set up to frighten the ignorant. The Pope in the

[1] "Marvel of Nations," pp. 174 and 175.

fourth century changed the law of God by changing the Sabbath to Sunday. This change is the mark of the beast; whoever after that keeps that law as thus changed is keeping not the law of God, but the Pope's law; is worshipping, not God, but the Pope. But all Christians for fifteen hundred years have kept Sunday, the Pope's Sabbath, the mark of the beast, and, as Smith says, were "*thereby marked* as followers of the power that made the change." From this conclusion there is no escape. And so all Sunday-keepers have had the mark of the beast, and have it now.

But they say that they do not teach that any one as yet has had the mark of the beast. This shows the absurdity of their argument. Sunday-keeping is the mark of the beast, yet Sunday-keepers have not got the mark of the beast! For instance: I have a hundred counterfeit bills; I pay them out to fifty men in Otsego, and they take and keep them, yet not a man of them has a counterfeit bill! Isn't that clear—as mud? But they don't know that they are counterfeit bills, and so are not guilty for having them. But have they not got counterfeit bills for all that? Certainly. So, if Sunday-keeping is the mark of the beast, then they have it whether they know it or not. God may not hold them guilty for it, but they have it just the same. Now, as soon as these fifty men are informed that their bills are counterfeit, are they not guilty if they use them after that? Yes. So, as soon as a man is informed that Sunday is the mark of the beast, if he keeps it after that has he not the mark of the beast as truly as ever he can have it? And if he still keeps Sunday voluntarily is he not just as guilty before God as though the law compelled him to keep it? Yes, and more so; because now he has no excuse, while then he could plead that he was compelled to do it. So, then, it needs no Sunday law to give men the mark of the beast. All Sunday-keepers have it already, and as soon as they are informed that Sunday is the mark of the beast, then they are guilty as worshippers of the beast. But Seventh-Day Adventists have already informed thousands upon this point. Then if they have not the mark of the beast, why not? Remember that Luther, Milton, Baxter, Bunyan and William Miller, father and founder of Adventism, were all informed on the Sabbath question, and still wrote against it and kept Sunday. Reader, this Advent mark of the beast is an absurdity and only a scarecrow. Don't be frightened.

Even if the Pope did change the Sabbath to Sunday, that would not make Sunday *his* mark. The mark of any person was that which he used to mark things as belonging to him. In Bible times a master would put his mark on the right hand or forehead of his slaves. Heathen gods had their worshippers marked so. This custom is referred to and used here as an illustration. So the worshippers of the beast would be required to do something which would mark or distinguish them as his followers. But keeping Sunday does not distinguish a Catholic from members of other Churches, for all Churches keep Sunday—the Greek, Armenian, Lutheran, Episcopal, Methodist, etc. The Pope has never used Sunday to distinguish his followers from others, nor as proof of his authority as head of the Church. He does point to the keys of St. Peter and his regular apostolic succession from him as proof of his authority. Says Dowling: "The Popes assert 'their *divine right* of supremacy in consequence of their claiming to be the successors of the Apostle Peter.'"[1] On this, not on Sunday-keeping, they base their claim of power. Some obscure writer is quoted, claiming authority for the Church to "command feasts and holy days," because that Church has made Sunday holy. This falls infinitely short of making Sunday the proof of all their authority, the one "mark" of that Church.

4. It is absurd to say that observing Sunday as the Sabbath is such a fearful crime as Adventists affirm. Hear Elder Smith: "Sunday-keeping must be the mark of the beast." "The reception of his mark must be something that involves the greatest offense that can be committed against God."[2] So keeping Sunday is more wicked than lying, stealing, or even murder or idolatry! Such a statement is monstrous. In the mind of any candid, thinking man, it must break down under the weight of its own absurdity.

[1] "History of Romanism," p. 44.
[2] "Marvel of Nations," pp. 170, 183.

WHAT, THEN, IS THE MARK OF THE BEAST?

What do Catholics themselves claim as the mark of the Papal Church? Do they say what it is? Yes, most emphatically. In every doctrinal book they publish, no matter how small, even a few paged catechism for little tots, up to a great cyclopedia of many volumes, this mark is always given in bold head-lines, thus:

"MARKS OF THE CHURCH"

Here is a sample from "A Shorter Catechism of the Catholic Religion":

"By what *marks* may the true Church of Christ be known?

"The true Church of Christ may be known by these four marks. She is (1) One; (2) Holy; (3) Catholic; (4) Apostolic.

"Which Church has all these four marks?

"It is plain that no Church has all these four marks except the Roman Catholic Church, that is, *the Church which acknowledges the Pope of Rome as the head*" (pages 37-38).

Here are the marks of that Church given exactly the same in every catechism and doctrinal work. Is Sunday-keeping one of them? No. It is never named in that list of marks. The crowning one of these is to acknowledge the authority of the Pope of Rome. So to acknowledge his supreme authority is to acknowledge that Church as the true Church. *Here you have the mark of the beast, if the Papacy is that beast!* Seventh-Day Adventists say that the "Beast" of Rev. xiii. 1–10 is the Papacy. Suppose we grant it. Then they say that Sunday-keeping is the "mark" of this beast, the Papacy. This we emphatically deny. The supreme mark, the one distinguishing characteristic of the Papacy, is the *supremacy of the Pope*. This one feature distinguishes it from all other churches. Thus Johnson's "New Universal Cyclopedia" says: "Roman Catholic Church, that body of Christians which acknowledges the authority of the Pope of Rome." Again in the same article it says: "The best summary of the leading articles of the Roman faith is contained in the creed of Pope Pius IV, which is binding upon all priests and public teachers, and which must be confessed by all converts." There are eleven articles. The tenth says: "I promise and swear true obedience to the Bishop of Rome, successor to St. Peter, Prince of the Apostles, and Vicar of Jesus Christ."

Every Catholic must take this oath. No one can become a member without it. Whoever confesses his adherence to this dogma thereby is *marked* as a papist, distinct from all other Churches. When he swears acceptance of this article, he thereby promises obedience to all the requirements of the Roman Church. Then is not this the *mark* of that Church? Surely.

Here are a few more quotations from Catholics on the same subject:

"The Church which Jesus Christ established may be defined briefly as a society composed of all who practice religion according to the guidance of His vicar (the Pope) on earth." [1]

"The whole Catholic world of more than two hundred and fifty millions of souls acknowledges and obeys the Pope, the Bishop of Rome, as the successor of St. Peter and the vicar of Christ on earth." [2]

Notice that all the time it is the supremacy of the Pope that is insisted upon as the one important mark of the true Church. It was a protest against this claim of the supremacy of the Pope that brought on the great Reformation under Luther and others. Thus Conway, a Catholic, in the "Question Box," says: "The Reformers of the sixteenth century, indeed, claimed a special mission to overthrow the existing government of the Church by denying the universal jurisdiction of the Pope" (page 187).

Yes, it was a protest against the supremacy of the Pope's authority which brought on the great Reformation. Hence, the name "Protestants."

Rome still urges the acknowledgment of this papal mark. As late as September 29, 1913, Cardinal Gibbons, in the *Baltimore American*, says:

"The reunion of the scattered branches of Christendom is a consummation to be devoutly wished. The *first* essential requirement is the recognition

---

[1] "Manual of Theology for the Laity," p. 185, by Rev. P. Geiermann.
[2] Same book, p. 233.

of the sovereign pontiff, who, as the successor of St. Peter, is the divinely appointed head of Christendom."

Notice that "*the first essential thing*" is to recognize the supremacy of the Pope. That is the one supreme question, the one test above all others. Accept that and all else will be easily settled! Of course, for that carries with it obedience to the whole papal system. Here you have the *mark* plainly enough.

"There must be a distinguishing characteristic which through all the differences of color, nationality, or education, will inevitably mark each adherent of that system and leave no question as to one's relation to it." A Catholic may be a loyal Englishman, an American, a Chinaman, a Japanese, a negro, or an Indian, no matter where he lives, or to what nation he belongs, the one person towards whom his fealty never wavers is "the Holy Father," the Pope of Rome.

Even Elder Smith, Adventist, says of this mark: "It will evidently be some act or acts by which men will be required to acknowledge the authority of that power (Papacy) and yield obedience to its mandates."[1] That is correct.

Every Catholic is required to do just exactly that, acknowledge the supremacy and infallibility of the Pope of Rome and yield implicit obedience to his authority and mandates. Does keeping Sunday do that?

[1] "Thoughts on Revelations," p. 591.

Here is a question. Mark it well. Does Rome ever require a person to promise to keep Sunday as a test of admittance as a member? Never! My neighbor is a Catholic in good standing, yet he works every Sunday. Could he deny the supremacy of the Pope and remain a member? No. Which, then, is the mark of loyalty to Rome? Is it Sunday-keeping? Even an Adventist must see the absurdity of that.

During the long night of papal supremacy hundreds of thousands were persecuted, their goods confiscated, themselves driven out to die as martyrs, because they would not acknowledge the supreme authority of the Pope. This is what all Protestants have been warring against for three hundred years and are doing it still. "The Supremacy of the Pope of Rome" has been the one disputed question in the history of the Church from the sixth century on till now. The great Eastern, or Greek, Church would never submit to it, and finally severed all connection with Rome on this very account. That issue is just as prominent to-day as ever. Protestant Churches protest against it now the same as then. Read our church papers; also the *Menace*, *Protestant Magazine*, etc.

If a man confesses his faith in the Roman pontiff as head of the Church and infallible, is he not counted by all as a Roman Catholic? Certainly. Now contrast this with Sunday-keeping. In my city there are Baptists, Methodists, Presbyterians, Congregationalists, Episcopalians, Disciples, Lutherans, United Brethren, and other Churches—all keeping Sunday. Does this mark them as Roman Catholics? Does any one think of them as papists on this account? Do they themselves ever think of it as marking them Catholics? Do the Catholics themselves count these as Catholics because they keep Sunday? Absolutely *no*. Every intelligent person knows that keeping Sunday does not mark any one as a papist. But to acknowledge the Pope as the infallible head of the Church does do this. Is not this absolutely true? Then what is the one universal mark of a Roman Catholic? Is it Sunday-keeping? We all know better. It is loyalty to the Pope of Rome. No candid man will deny that. Every Catholic authority will agree with it. Here, then, is the "mark" of the Papacy.

What is the one characteristic mark of a Mohammedan? It is loyalty to Mohammed as God's prophet. What of a Christian Scientist? Loyalty to Mrs. Eddy as head of that Church. What of a Christian? Loyalty to Christ as the head of the Church. What, then, is the chief mark of a papist? Loyalty to the Pope, "the Holy Father," as the supreme infallible head of the Papacy. Every Catholic will say that. Here is the mark of the beast, if the Papacy is the beast as Adventists claim.

XII

THE TEN COMMANDMENTS NOT CHANGED BY CATHOLICS—ADVENTISTS DECAPITATE THE DECALOGUE

SEVENTH-DAY ADVENTISTS say that the Catholic Church has cut out the second one, the one against images, has changed the Sabbath precept, and divided the tenth one into two to make up the ten. How do they try to prove this? They quote from Catholic catechisms, small ones, where only a few words of the longer commandments are given, while the rest is omitted. The short ones are given in full and our tenth divided into two. Then they compare these commandments in the Catholic *catechisms* with those in our *Bible*. Is this fair? No. They should compare the commandments in Catholic Bibles with those in our Bibles, and those in Catholic catechisms with those in Protestant catechisms. This is the only fair way. If they did this, they would find no material difference in either. I have both Bibles before me. Opening to Exodus xx. all the ten commandments, every word of each one, images, Sabbath, the tenth, and all, are given in full in the Catholic Bible; not a word is omitted. Get one and see for yourself.

Now compare Catholic catechisms with Protestant catechisms. Is there any material difference between them in quoting the commandments? None at all. In order to be sure on this point, I have spent much time to thoroughly investigate it. I have gathered a large number of Catholic catechisms. Have them here now. Then have gone to the pastors of many Protestant Churches, as Baptist, Episcopal, Presbyterian, Lutheran, Dutch Reformed, etc., and have examined their catechisms. In all these I find they have done practically the same as the Catholics have. In the Protestant catechism for small children, generally only a few words from the long commandments are given, while the short ones are given in full. This is to save space and memorizing. The Catholics have done the same thing and for the same reason. Then each Church, Protestant or Catholic, explains these their way; but the commandments themselves are given as full in one as in the other.

On one side of my home is a Catholic family, on the other side is a Protestant family—Lutheran. I borrowed catechisms of both. Here are the ten commandments in the small Catholic catechism:

"Say the ten commandments.

"I. I am the Lord thy God, who brought thee out of the land of Egypt, out of the house of bondage. Thou shalt have no strange gods before me; thou shalt not make to thyself any graven thing, nor the likeness of anything that is in the heaven above, or in the earth beneath, or in the waters under the earth. Thou shalt not adore them nor serve them.

DECALOGUE NOT CHANGED BY CATHOLICS 249

"II. Thou shalt not take the name of the Lord thy God in vain.

"III. Remember that thou keep holy the Sabbath day.

"IV. Honor thy father and thy mother that it may be well with thee, and thou mayest live long on the earth.

"V. Thou shalt not kill.

"VI. Thou shalt not commit adultery.

"VII. Thou shalt not steal.

"VIII. Thou shalt not bear false witness against thy neighbor.

"IX. Thou shalt not covet thy neighbor's wife.

"X. Thou shalt not covet thy neighbor's goods."

Notice here that Catholics include in the first commandment what we call the second commandment. Then our tenth is divided into two. Lutherans divide them just the same way. Further on I will give the reason for this. Observe that the command against images is given in full. And this is a small Catholic catechism used by my neighbor.

Now here are the commandments as given in the small catechism used by my Lutheran neighbor, a Protestant:

"I. I am the Lord thy God. Thou shalt have no other gods before me.

"II. Thou shalt not take the name of the Lord thy God in vain.

"III. Thou shalt keep the Sabbath day holy.

"IV. Honor thy father and thy mother that

thou mayest live long upon the land which the Lord thy God giveth thee.

"V. Thou shalt not kill.

"VI. Thou shalt not commit adultery.

"VII. Thou shalt not steal.

"VIII. Thou shalt not bear false witness against thy neighbor.

"IX. Thou shalt not covet thy neighbor's house.

"X. Thou shalt not covet thy neighbor's wife, nor his man-servant, nor his maid-servant, nor his ox, nor his ass, nor anything that is thy neighbor's."

Notice in this Protestant catechism that our second commandment is omitted entirely. Why? Was it to get rid of that one because it forbid images? No, for Lutherans use no images, but oppose them. They include our second in their first, the same as do Catholics. So they give only the first words and omit the long explanation. That is all. Then the tenth is divided into two, the same as the Catholic. None of this was done, whether by Lutherans or Catholics, to "mutilate the law of God," as Adventists say. It is one of the ways of dividing them, that is all. (See explanation and table at close of this chapter.)

My Catholic neighbor, mentioned above, also loaned me a larger catechism which his daughter studies in the Catholic high school here. It is entitled, "A Full Course of Instruction in Explanation of the Catechism, by Rev. J. Perry, for Colleges, Academies, and Private Families. Endorsed by the Archbishop of St. Louis." Notice, this is used in high schools, colleges, academies, and families. Beginning on page 151, there are fifty-nine pages given to the ten commandments. Each one is given in full. The first one begins, and properly too, with "I am the Lord thy God," etc. Then all, every word, of our first and second commandments, is given in the first one; not a word against images is omitted.

Coming to the Sabbath precept, our fourth, but their third, I read: "Recite the full text of the third commandment." Then every word of the Sabbath precept is given in full, not a word omitted or changed, and so of the whole ten. Obedience to each of these is taught as Catholics understand them.

What now becomes of the assertion that Catholics have "mutilated the law of God" or have expunged one of the ten commandments? It is not the truth. All that can be truthfully said is that they explain them differently from what Protestants do. But they believe in them all, teach all of them and print all of them in full in their Bibles and in their larger catechisms. In their small catechisms they do just as Protestants do in their small ones, viz., give a few words of each. Hence it is unfair to compare these little catechisms with the whole law in our Bible.

Roman priests are guilty of withholding the entire Bible from their people, so that the great mass of them never see a Bible. When priests do quote the Bible, they quote it correctly enough, but explain it to suit Romanism. They quote the precepts about images and the Sabbath correctly, but explain both to fit their views. As they are accused of breaking the second commandment by the use of images, they are careful, as seen above, to put in every word of that precept even in their small catechisms. Then, of course, they have to explain it all away. They have perverted the entire Gospel as well as the Old Testament.

Neither the Popes nor the Roman Church had anything to do with dividing the Decalogue. Every word of the ten commandments is given whichever way they are divided.

It should be remembered that in the Hebrew, in which the Decalogue was written, the words all ran right along together. There were no marks whatever between the words or the commandments. Hence all were left to divide them as each judged nearest correct. So it happened that they were divided differently, that is all.

THE CATHOLIC DIVISION OF THE DECALOGUE

Seventh-Day Adventists have made a great ado over the way Catholics divide and number the ten commandments. They have gotten up a chart showing in one column the Decalogue " as changed by the Pope " and in another as " given by God." Here they show how " the Pope has changed God's law in fulfillment of Dan. vii. 25." According to this, the Catholics included in the first commandment what we have in the first two. Then our third is their second, our fourth their third, and so on till our tenth, of which they make two. Adventists claim that the Pope did this to get rid of the second commandment and to change the Sabbath. But the whole thing is utterly false, as may be seen under the word decalogue in any religious encyclopedia. The "Schaff-Herzog Encyclopedia" says:

"There have been three arrangements of the Decalogue—the Talmudic (Jewish), the Augustinian (adopted by the Roman Catholic and Lutheran Churches), and the Hellenistic (Greek), the view of Philo, Josephus, Origen, the Greek and Reformed Churches, etc. The following table exhibits the differences, the record in Exodus xx. being used.

TALMUDIC	HELLENISTIC	AUGUSTINIAN
1. I am the Lord, etc. (v. 2).	1. Against Idols, (v. 3).	1. Against idols and images, (3-6).
2. Against Idols and images, (3-6).	2. Against images, (4-6).	2. Blasphemy.
3. Blasphemy.	3. Blasphemy.	3. The Sabbath.
4. The Sabbath.	4. The Sabbath.	4. Filial Obedience.
5. Filial Obedience.	5. Filial Obedience.	5. Murder.
6. Murder.	6. Murder.	6. Adultery.
7. Adultery.	7. Adultery.	7. Theft.
8. Theft.	8. Theft.	8. False witness.
9. False witness.	9. False witness.	9. Thou shalt not covet thy neighbor's h. (17).
10. Coveting.	10. Coveting.	10. The rest of v. 17.

It will be seen here that the Catholics have simply followed Augustine, one of the early Fathers, in this, while we have followed the Greeks.

Augustine, A. D. 353-430, was neither a Pope nor a papist. Next to Paul, he was the most devoted and renowned minister Christianity ever produced. He had the most profound reverence for the Holy Scriptures. The Catholics and Lutherans have followed his division of the Decalogue. Hence this division was not made by a Pope nor by the Papacy. A little investigation of facts exposes the weakness of many of the Sabbatarian arguments like this one.

THE DECALOGUE DECAPITATED

Strange as it may seem, Adventists themselves are the ones who "mutilate" the commandments. They leave off the most important part of the Decalogue, viz., that part which tells who gave the law, when it was given, and to whom given. Consulting a lawyer, he tells me that every law passed by a state, or by the United States, in order to be of binding force, must begin with what is called, "The Enacting Clause." Thus, opening to a law passed by the legislature of Michigan, February 16, 1882, I read: "Be it enacted by the senate and house of representatives of the State of Michigan," etc. Then follows the body of the law of which this "enacting clause" is a necessary part. That introductory clause tells who gave the law, when it was given, and to whom given. Leave these words off and the law is a dead letter.

Exactly so with the Decalogue. The enacting clause is there in plain words.

Let us examine it. Moses says distinctly that all the words which the Lord spoke were written on the tables of stone: " And the Lord delivered unto me two tables of stone, written with the finger of God: and on them was written according to all the words which the Lord spake with you in the Mount, out of the midst of the fire" (Deut. ix. 10). This text is too decisive to be evaded. All that God spoke was written on the tables and was a part of the Decalogue. Here are the first words: "And God spake all these words, saying, I am the Lord, thy God, which brought thee out of the land of Egypt, out of the house of bondage. Thou shalt have no other gods before Me," etc. (Ex. xx. 1–3). These words are as much a part of the Decalogue as any of the rest of it. They were spoken by God from heaven, written by His finger, were engraven on the stone, and put in the ark.

Adventists urge that the ten commandments are of higher importance than other parts of the law, because they were spoken directly by God's own voice, written with His finger, engraved on stone, put in the ark and placed in the Most Holy Place. Very well. All this is true of these words in the enacting clause, or first words. These words were spoken by God, written by God, engraved on the stone, put in the ark, and then in the Most Holy Place just the same as all the rest of the commandments. Hence one is as sacred as the other and all should be kept together. These explain directly who the author of that law is, viz., The Lord thy God that brought thee out of Egyptian bondage. Nothing could be plainer. They should be left where God put them.

Now look at the law chart which the Seventh-Day Adventists hang up as the "Law of God."

Are these words on there? No, indeed. They are left off. If put on, they would spoil their whole theory of that law.

They assert that the Sabbath precept is the only thing in the Decalogue that tells who gave it. Thus: "Aside from this precept [the Sabbath] there is nothing in the Decalogue to show by whose authority the law is given."[1]

This is not true. The opening words of that law, "the enacting clause," tell as plainly as words can tell who gave it, when it was given, and to whom given. See how clear it is: "I am the Lord thy God that brought thee out of Egypt. Thou shalt have no other gods before Me." To whom does "Me" refer? Only one answer can be given: It refers to the Lord God who has just spoken. He first tells them who He is, and then all the commandments that follow are given on His authority.

But Adventists mutilate the law by cutting the head right off, by leaving off the enacting clause, and then assert that there is nothing in the Decalogue except the Sabbath precept to tell who gave that law! Is not this misleading?

Take an audience of one hundred people, hang up the law chart as Adventists print it with the introductory words left off, and how many of the audience would notice the omission? Few, if any at all. The preacher then asserts that there is nothing in that law except the Sabbath precept to

[1] Mrs. White, in "Great Controversy," p. 284.

tell who gave the law! No wonder people are misled. In the second copy of the law given in Deut. v. 1-22 all reference to creation is omitted while every word of the enacting clause is on there. This shows that deliverance from Egypt was the authority on which that law was made. Adventists accuse Catholics of mutilating the Decalogue. It is exactly the other way. Catholics include all the introductory words in the first commandment, and then give the whole together. Thus "A Study of the Catholic Religion," by Rev. Chas. Coppens, page 283: "The first commandment is thus: 'I am the Lord thy God who brought thee out of the land of Egypt, out of the house of bondage. Thou shalt not have strange gods before Me,'" etc. You see Catholics always include all the enacting clause in the first commandment, just as should be done. In every Catholic catechism or doctrinal book when the commandments are quoted they all begin the same way with these words, just as God Himself began them: "I am the Lord thy God that brought thee out of Egypt." There are two hundred and fifty million Catholics, half of Christendom, who all quote the commandments that way. So also the entire Greek Orthodox Catholic Church, numbering one hundred and fifty millions, all include those words in the first commandment. I went to their priest and he showed me how they quote them. Then all the Lutherans, fifty millions, do the same. Then all the Jewish people, fourteen millions, do the same. So over five hundred million believers in the Bible all include those words in the first commandment. But Adventists leave off these words.

Leaving all the words of the ten commandments on just as God gave them spoils the argument that the Sabbath is the seal of the law. To prove this they assert that there is nothing else in that law that tells who gave it. But the first words tell who gave it. This squarely contradicts their position, as is readily seen.

I call on them to throw away their old charts of the ten commandments and print them just as God gave them.

Evidently originally the Adventists did not leave off these important words with the purpose of deceiving. Elders White, Bates, Rhodes, etc., the first leaders, were not scholarly men. In printing the law chart, they simply copied it after those used by the Episcopal Church and others in church service. By them the words were omitted to save length in repeating. While I was an Adventist minister I have, hundreds of times, preached from that law chart and argued just as they do now with no thought of deceiving. I simply did not then know any better, nor do most of them now. But their intelligent leaders should know better, because, for over twenty years past, I have called their attention to this unfair omission which plainly contradicts the argument that the Sabbath precept is the only thing that tells who gave the law.

"HE SHALL THINK TO CHANGE TIMES AND LAWS"—*Dan. vii. 25.*

Seventh-Day Adventists make great capital of this text. They argue that it means the Pope, or Papacy. Then they claim that the Papacy changed the Sabbath, the fourth commandment, and thus fulfilled this prophecy. To this we object. In Chapter VI we have proved that the change in the day was made in the Apostolic Church, hundreds of years before there was any Papacy. In Chapter VII we have shown that the change in the day was made in the Eastern Church, where the Papacy never ruled.

The wording of Dan. vii. 25 shows that the text has a far wider meaning than merely changing the Sabbath. It was to change "times and laws"—both plural. To change the Sabbath would only be changing one time and one law. This would not fulfill the prophecy. But the Papacy has changed numerous "times and laws." Read the following from "Systematic Study of the Catholic Religion," by Chas. Coppens, page 318:

"THE COMMANDMENTS OF THE CHURCH

"The laws enacted by the Church, in order to guide her members to eternal salvation, are *many and numerous*. They are contained in her Canon Law."

Then follows a long list of holy "times" and church "laws" which are not in the Bible, and these times and laws have been changed time and again through the centuries. (See any commentary on Dan. vii. 25.)

The Roman Church has fulfilled this prophecy many times over outside of any reference to the Sabbath.

The Pope claims the right to change or annul the laws of beings or states and has often done so. He decrees holy days and holy times, then changes them at his will. All this has been prominent in the history of the Papacy during the Dark Ages. This has amply fulfilled the prophecy without any reference to the Sabbath.

This text, Dan. vii. 25, is the one on which Adventists rely to prove that the Papacy has changed the Sabbath. They quote it on all occasions as proof positive on this point. But the careful reader will notice that they have to read into the text what the Lord omitted to put there. The Sabbath is in no way mentioned in the text. They have to go a long way and assume much to even make their theory look plausible.

Just so Rev. xiv. 12, "Here are they that keep the commandments of God," is their great text to prove that the Sabbath is to be restored by them now. But here again they put in what the Lord left out—the Sabbath.

If the Lord meant the Sabbath in both texts why did He not say so instead of leaving it for Adventists to insert later? They make these texts play the tune which fits their theory, that is all.

Appendix A

SUNDAY CIVIL LAWS CONSTITUTIONAL

SEVENTH-DAY ADVENTISTS assert that all Sunday laws are unconstitutional because the constitution forbids making any law concerning the establishment of religion. But a civil law restricting labor on Sunday has nothing to do with establishing religion. It is simply the exercise of the "police power" given to every state. The Supreme Court of the United States is the highest authority in our nation. It has repeatedly declared civil Sunday laws constitutional. In 1895 (Hennington vs. Georgia) the court said: "The legislature having the power to enact laws to secure the comfort, happiness, and health of the people, it was within its discretion to fix the day when all labor within the limits of the State, works of necessity and charity excepted, should cease."

Again in 1884 the same high court said, The Sunday law is not "a religious regulation, but is the legitimate exercise of the police power, and is itself a police regulation. The day of rest ordinance by the state is a civil, not a religious, institution."

Later, Song Hing vs. Crowly, said: "Laws setting aside Sunday as a day of rest should be upheld, not from any right of the Government to legislate for the promotion of religious observances, but from its right to protect all citizens from the physical and moral debasement which comes from uninterrupted labor."

Similar decisions upholding Sunday laws as civil police regulations have been rendered by the Supreme Courts of a large number of states, as Georgia, South Carolina, Ohio, New York, Massachusetts, West Virginia, Illinois, Louisiana, Maryland, Kansas, etc.

These impartial high courts are far better judges of what is constitutional than are partisan Adventists. In their selfish zeal to oppose all Sunday regulations, Adventists go beyond the truth and contradict the highest legal authorities in the United States.

BIBLIOLIFE

Old Books Deserve a New Life
www.bibliolife.com

Did you know that you can get most of our titles in our trademark **EasyScript**™ print format? **EasyScript**™ provides readers with a larger than average typeface, for a reading experience that's easier on the eyes.

Did you know that we have an ever-growing collection of books in many languages?

Order online:
www.bibliolife.com/store

Or to exclusively browse our **EasyScript**™ collection:
www.bibliogrande.com

At BiblioLife, we aim to make knowledge more accessible by making thousands of titles available to you – quickly and affordably.

Contact us:
BiblioLife
PO Box 21206
Charleston, SC 29413

CPSIA information can be obtained at www.ICGtesting.com
Printed in the USA
LVOW131825020212

266766LV00014B/1/P